Village Life

in Late Tsarist Russia

Indiana-Michigan Series in Russian and East European Studies

Alexander Rabinowitch and William G. Rosenberg, general editors

Village Life
in Late Tsarist Russia

by
OLGA SEMYONOVA TIAN-SHANSKAIA

EDITED BY DAVID L. RANSEL
Translated by David L. Ransel with Michael Levine

Indiana
University
Press
BLOOMINGTON AND INDIANAPOLIS

INDIANA UNIVERSITY PRESS
601 NORTH MORTON STREET
BLOOMINGTON, IN 47404-3797 USA

HTTP://IUPRESS.INDIANA.EDU

Telephone orders 800-842-6796
Fax orders 812-855-7931
Orders by e-mail iuporder@indiana.edu

The paper used in this publication meets the minimum requirements of American National Standard for Information Sciences—Permanence of Paper for Printed Library Materials, ANSI Z39.48-1984.

Manufactured in the United States of America

Library of Congress Cataloging-in-Publication Data

Semyonova Tian-Shanskaia, Olga, 1863–1906.
Village life in late tsarist Russia : an ethnography by Olga Semyonova Tian-Shanskaia / edited by David L. Ransel : translated by David L. Ransel, with Michael Levine.
p. cm. — (Indiana-Michigan series in Russian and East European studies)
Translated from Russian.
Includes bibliographical references.
ISBN 978-0-253-34797-8 (alk. paper). — ISBN 978-0-253-20784-5 (pbk.)
1. Russia—Rural conditions. 2. Russia—Social conditions—1801–1917. 3. Villages—Russia—History—19th century. 4. Sex customs—Russia—History—19th century. I. Ransel, David L. II. Title. III. Series.
HN523.S46 1993
307.72'0947—dc20 92-28558

8 9 10 11 12 13 12 11 10 09 08

CONTENTS

ACKNOWLEDGMENTS

This project has been assisted by support from a number of foundations and individuals. A Mellon Grant through the Russian and East European Institute of Indiana University paid Michael Levine for his collaboration in the translation. During 1989-1990, when I received funding from the Guggenheim Foundation, the International Research and Exchanges Board (IREX), and a Fulbright-Hays fellowship, I was able to devote a portion of my time to this project, in particular the work in Russian archives. I am grateful to the donors and staffs of these funding agencies for their generous support.

Several individuals contributed important advice. Professors Nadya Peterson of the University of Pennsylvania, Nina Perlina of Indiana University, and Yelena Stepanova of Yekaterinburg Technical University helped me understand some difficult phrases in Russian, especially in the expressions of the peasants. Professor Linda Ivanits of Pennsylvania State University advised on some of the folkloric terms; Olga Melnikova, a curator in the Kremlin museum, provided crucial information on the Semyonov Tian-Shanskii family from archives that I was unable to consult (I acknowledge her help again in the specific footnote references that she gave me). Materials from the Academy of Sciences Archive in St. Petersburg came to me through the mediation of Aleksandr Isupov, an advanced graduate student at St. Petersburg University. Professor Janet Kennedy and Mr. Eli Weinerman, both at Indiana University, helped with references and advice on pictures. Special appreciation goes to T. M. Pankova of the Riazan Historical-Architectural Museum in the city of Riazan for selecting from the museum's photo archive many of the pictures used in this book, and to Ben Eklof and Molly Pyle for facilitating their delivery. Professor Ellen Dwyer of Indiana University took a sharp editorial pen to the introduction, and Professor Steven L. Hoch of the University of Iowa offered a number of valuable suggestions for improvement of both the introduction and the translation. To all these people, and to my wife Terry for her patience and understanding, I am most thankful.

Note on the Text

I have used the Library of Congress system of transliteration throughout; however, some minor modifications have been made in the text so that readers unfamiliar with Russian can approximate the correct pronunciation of names and terms. For example, the Russian letter *ё* has been rendered as *yo;* soft vowels are rendered as *ya, yu,* and *ye* at the beginning of a word, and as *ia, iu,* and *e* elsewhere. Soft signs have been omitted from transliterated Russian first names in the body of the book but retained in the notes for proper reference.

ABBREVIATIONS

AGO AN SSSR	Archive of the Russian Geographical Society, St. Petersburg
Arkhiv AN SSSR	Archive of the Russian Academy of Sciences, St. Petersburg branch
LGALI	The Leningrad State Archive of Literature and Art

INTRODUCTION

Russia in the late nineteenth century was a society in crisis. For some, the pace of development was too slow. Germany, France, England, and the United States—the countries to which most educated Russians instinctively compared their own—were well ahead of Russia in industrialization and urbanization, and they had a far higher level of general education and culture. For others, change was too rapid. They blamed the government's drive to catch up with the West for the increasingly deep fissures in society, which seemed to threaten the country with revolution. Yet, however educated Russians may have viewed the sources of the crisis, most believed that its resolution depended ultimately on the attitudes and actions of the common people, the peasants, who constituted about 85 percent of the nation's population. Peasants not only were rural dwellers, but they also, as migrant laborers in the cities and factory towns, made up the majority of the industrial working class. As peasants in uniform, they composed the bulk of the armed forces. Curiously enough, both radical critics of the established regime and its conservative defenders, despite their differences with one another and their shared ignorance of village life, were convinced that they knew what the common people wanted and needed and could speak in their name. As a consequence, discussion of peasants and of Russia's future, an important part of public discourse in late tsarist Russia, was filled with a great many myths and misconceptions.

The study that follows was undertaken by its author, Olga Petrovna Semyonova Tian-Shanskaia, and her collaborator, K. V. Nikolaevskii, in the late 1890s in order to meet the need for information about the actual life conditions, attitudes, and aspirations of the peasantry. The two best-known accounts of peasant life then available (both imprints of the 1880s) were A. N. Engelgardt's *From the Village: Twelve Letters, 1872–1887* and A. Yefimenko's *Studies of Peasant Life*. The first was a literary work, a series of

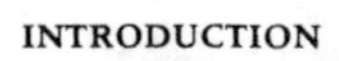

Olga Semyonova Tian-Shanskaia

letters published over many years in a major Russian magazine, which focused largely on the rural economy and on the relationship of peasants and noble landlords in organizing it. The Yefimenko study went into more aspects of peasant life, including family life and customs, but presented information in a static and abstract form that failed to capture the fluidity and variability of village life. I should add that at the same time that Semyonova (I use the short form of her name for convenience) and Nikolaevskii began their work, a major national survey of peasant life was launched by the private ethnographic bureau established by a wealthy noble, V. N. Tenishev. The bureau distributed a questionnaire with several hundred items to priests, school teachers, amateur ethnographers, and other literate inhabitants of villages throughout the Russian empire. The responses constitute the richest single fund of information on peasant life from the late nineteenth century and have been used in scholarly studies of folklore, language, folk medicine, and other topics. But there is no single work based on this collection or otherwise produced that offers the intimate portrayal of peasant family life, sexual mores, and the treatment of women that we find in Semyonova's study.

This unusual accomplishment stems from Semyonova's pioneering approach to peasant life through intensive, lengthy study of one community. Even the leaders of the English school of ethnography, the first to develop and "codify" the practice of intimate field-work contacts in the early decades of this century, still relied heavily in the late nineteenth century on information gathered through questionnaires sent to missionaries and colonial officials. On their few excursions into the field, the ethnographers remained onboard a ship anchored offshore or on the veranda of the local colonial office and made notes on the basis of reports brought to them by local informants. As often as not, the informants were traders or other outsiders in regular contact with native populations, not the natives themselves. Visits were brief, for the objective was to survey a large range of peoples in order to verify hypotheses about the diffusion throughout the world of ancient customs. Not until the 1910s did British ethnographers set up camp in a village for months on end and become "participant observers" of everyday life. The most daring and original of these was Bronislaw Malinowski, whose work set the standard for subsequent generations.[1]

In this respect, Semyonova was ahead of her time. She and Nikolaevskii began by designing a research program based on an extensive list of questions about the economic, social, and family life of the peasantry. Semyonova then sought answers to the questions in the course of four years of observation (1898 to 1902) in villages close to her family estate in the Dankov district of Riazan province. As her collaborator Nikolaevskii pointed out in a letter written in late 1906, "the aim of the project was to portray a peasant of average intelligence, economic status, and moral character from the Black Earth region of Russia at the turn of the century. The political and social climate of that time (as is still true today) was such that everyone expected that the peasant alone would be able to bring about a new order in Russia, and the pace of this change was also entirely dependent on the peasantry. It stood to reason, therefore, that this average peasant 'Ivan' would have been, or better, ought to have been, an object of interest to everyone, whereas in actuality the image of this Ivan remained not merely vague but altogether unknown." Nikolaevskii went on to say that the project was to encompass the entire life of Ivan from birth to maturity. Their questions "focused chiefly on economic and social conditions and were intended to bring in issues of everyday life only to the extent that they illuminated the economic and social conditions."[2] For them, "social conditions" covered a broad range of topics, including birth, courtship, marriage, mores, religious outlook, and consciousness. By producing a "realistic"

1. For background, see the essays in *Observers Observed: Essays on Ethnographic Fieldwork*, ed. George W. Stocking, Jr. (History of Anthropology, vol. 1) (Madison: University of Wisconsin Press, 1983).

2. K. V. Nikolaevskii to Varvara Petrovna Shneider (December 2, 1906), AGO, fond 109, opis' 1, chast' 1, delo 170, ll. 1–2. The letter was written just after Semyonova's death, evidently to provide information for Shneider's published eulogy (cited in footnote 4), in which a portion of the letter was quoted.

portrayal of Ivan, Semyonova and Nikolaevskii hoped to combat the naive but widely accepted ideas of populist writers who believed that Russian peasants were naturally cooperative and communitarian and could therefore provide a native foundation for Russian socialism.

Semyonova failed to provide a clear guide to the villages she was studying and merely refers to one or another of them from time to time. At the center of her study is the village of Muraevnia, known in Russian as a *selo,* that is, a village large enough to have its own church. Muraevnia was a substantial community, consisting of just over two thousand inhabitants at the turn of the century. Most of its homes were built of brick, and it boasted a "two-class school," an institution that provided five years of schooling in two classrooms, plus a school for girls and women, which evidently taught crafts such as lacemaking (a local specialty) and some general education. Muraevnia was situated on the Ranova River about one kilometer upstream from Semyonova's family estate of "Gremiachka." (See the map on page xvi.) She also mentions events and conditions in other villages in the vicinity: Zabolot'e and Ol'khi, Kobel'sha, Sergeevka, Chernyshevka, and Karavaevo. The first two, which lay close together about four kilometers upriver from Muraevnia, formed a single census unit with twenty-four hundred inhabitants.[3] This community, like Muraevnia, dwarfed some of the other villages Semyonova mentions, which she describes as having only fifteen homes (or about one hundred inhabitants).

After finishing her formal field work in 1902, Semyonova continued to rework her notes until her death in 1906, hoping to add observations about the impact on her villages of the civil disturbances leading up to and connected with the revolutionary years of 1905–1906.[4] She did not, however, succeed in synthesizing all her materials. She had long suffered from a heart condition,

3. V. P. Semenov, ed., *Rossiia. Polnoe geograficheskoe opisanie nashego otechestva,* vol. 2: *Srednerusskaia chernozemnaia oblast'* (St. Petersburg, 1902), 407.
4. V. P. Shneider, "Pamiati Ol'gi Petrovny Semenovoi," *Izvestiia imperatorskogo russkogo geograficheskogo obshchestva,* vol. 43 (1907), 48.

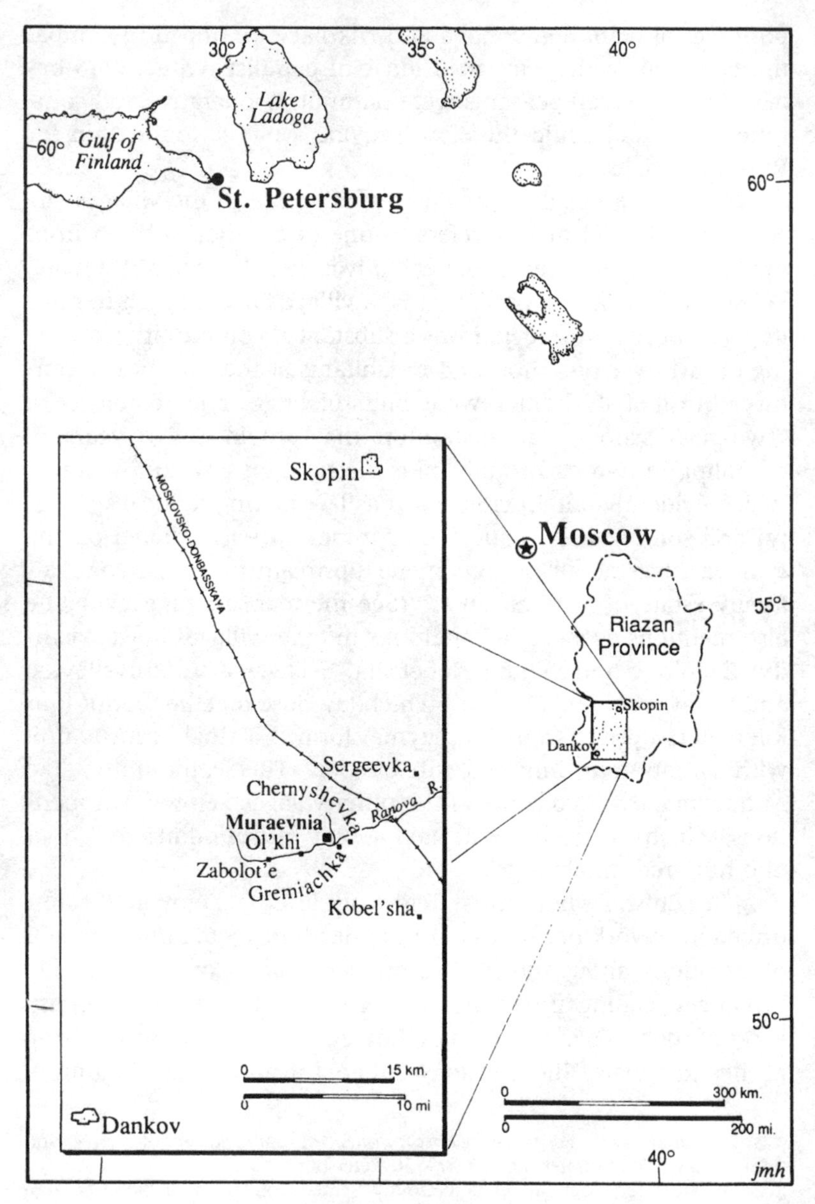
30°
35°
40°
60°
Lake Ladoga
Gulf of Finland
St. Petersburg
60°
Moscow
55°
Riazan Province
Skopin
Dankov
50°
0
300 km.
0
200 mi.
40°
jmh
Skopin
MOSKOVSKO-DONBASSKAYA
Sergeevka
Chernyshevka
Ranova R.
Muraevnia
Ol'khi
Zabolot'e
Gremiachka
Kobel'sha
0
15 km.
0
10 mi
Dankov

evidently the result of rheumatic fever, for which she took heavy doses of digitalis.[5] Her cousin Vera Dmitrievna reported in her unpublished memoirs that in the last months of her life Olga Semyonova was unable to walk because of the swelling of her legs and sat alone in her room, hiding her condition from relatives and doctors.[6] The swelling suggests that she was suffering from dropsy and probably died from this condition or its associated infections, pneumonias, septic emboli, and endocarditis.[7] She was forty-three years old. At her death, the project remained unfinished, consisting of a first draft of the composite picture of "Ivan" up to the time of his marriage and a series of unconnected field notes and vignettes from peasant life.

Semyonova's study was edited by her friend Varvara Shneider and published eight years after her death by the Imperial Russian Geographical Society, under the title *The Life of "Ivan": Sketches of Peasant Life from One of the Black Earth Provinces.*[8] Perhaps because of its appearance in 1914, at the start of seven years of war, revolution, and civil war, the work was lost sight of by all but a few specialists in ethnography and the history of peasant institutions. Its neglect may also be attributable to the poor organization of the original text, much of which remained a series of unintegrated vignettes. Even in the composite picture of "Ivan" at the start of the book, materials were introduced chaotically, with observations on a particular subject scattered here and there.

5. A surviving relative, Anastasia ("Stana") Mikhailovna Semyonova Tian-Shanskaia (1913–1992), with whom I spoke in 1990, told me that it was this medicine that finally killed her. But, as noted below, the reported symptoms could support a number of diagnoses.
6. I am grateful to Olga Melnikova for giving me this reference and the information about Olga Semyonova. The memoirs in question are held in LGALI, f. 116, op. 1, ed. khr. 11.
7. With regard to the link of rheumatic fever and dropsy and their fatal effects, see Ann G. Carmichael, "The Health Status of Florentines in the Fifteenth Century," in *Life and Death in Fifteenth-Century Florence*, ed. Marcel Tetel, Ronald Witt, and Rona Goffen (Durham, N.C.: Duke University Press, 1989), esp. 39, 42-43.
8. *Zhizn' "Ivana": Ocherki iz byta krest'ian odnoi iz chernozemnykh gubernii*, published as volume 39 of the *Zapiski imperatorskogo russkogo geograficheskogo obshchestva po otdeleniiu etnografii* (St. Petersburg, 1914).

Issues were taken up briefly, dropped, and then returned to later for further development. In constructing this translated text, therefore, I have been very free in moving elements of the original around, taking paragraphs and sometimes even sentences from widely dispersed points and patching them into other places in the text, or even building new paragraphs and sections out of scattered remnants. In addition, I have woven into this much-reorganized text a number of long and short passages found in the author's personal archives (mainly undigested field notes from two St. Petersburg repositories) and from notes of hers published by her friend Varvara Shneider in a eulogy that appeared in 1906 in a periodical of the Russian Geographic Society. All these additions to the original text are signaled in footnotes at the point they appear, and archival or other references are provided. The chapter breakdown, headings, introductory notes, and footnotes in this English version are my own (with the exception of a couple of footnotes by Semyonova, identified by placement of her last name in brackets at their close), as is the title, *Village Life in Late Tsarist Russia*.

Before reading an ethnography, one should learn about the author. Ethnographers such as Semyonova undertake their researches for a variety of reasons, and the particular stance, or frame of reference, of each researcher bears on the results. The frame of reference is constituted by the researcher's position in time, professional and political commitments, psychology, training, and other factors. Ethnography begins with the awareness of difference, and the ethnographer, on the basis of his or her frame of reference and available language and images, must decide how to represent the object of study. It is important, therefore, to assess Semyonova's position in relation to the peasants she tells us about. Unfortunately, the Russian publishers of Semyonova's original text did not write much about her as a person. What I have been able to learn about her comes from a variety of sources, including the eulogy by Varvara Shneider mentioned earlier, references in a few published and unpublished diaries, and two short conversations with her surviving relatives.

Born in 1863 into a prominent scientific family, Olga Semyonova was the daughter of the famous explorer, geographer, and statistician Pyotr Petrovich Semyonov (later given the addition Tian-Shanskii by the emperor in recognition of his explorations of the Tien Shan mountains of Central Asia). Her father also played a major role in designing the legislation for the emancipation of the Russian peasants from serfdom, a reform implemented in the years 1861–1863. Although Semyonova lived half of her life in St. Petersburg and traveled abroad for a time with her family, she often spent her summers at "Gremiachka," the family estate in Riazan province close to the villages where she later carried out her study of peasant life. She seemed to have inherited much of her father's spirit of exploration and inquiry; at the time of her death, her nephew Leonid, a well-known writer and Tolstoyan philosopher, wrote of the aunt "so dear to me": "She died in the prime of life, not satisfied with anything, hungry for knowledge, seeking [truth]."[9]

Semyonova's adult life was marked by personal tragedy. According to her relative Anastasia Mikhailovna, when an "unworthy" young man fell in love with Olga, she dismissed his offer of marriage.[10] Subsequently, the rejected suitor shot himself in the head and died.[11] Semyonova thereafter refused to consider marriage, withdrew increasingly from the social and intellectual life of the capital, and began to spend more time on the family estate, where she became acquainted with every family in the collection of villages that was associated with it.

Semyonova produced her first important ethnographic study in 1886 at the age of twenty-three—a collection of folk songs from Riazan province, which won her a silver medal from the Imperial

9. L. D. Semenov Tian'-Shanskii, "Zapiski. Greshnyi greshnym," *Uchenye zapiski Tartuskogo universiteta*, vol. 414 (Tartu, 1977), 136.

10. Anastasia Mikhailovna refused to explain more about the man in question and indicated that no one in the family was permitted to talk about the affair.

11. This information comes, again, from the unpublished memoirs of Vera Dmitrievna, cited earlier, thanks to Olga Melnikova.

Russian Geographical Society.[12] She continued collecting peasant songs to the end of her life; brief excerpts of some of them appear in the work translated here. Another major work by Semyonova, done in collaboration with her brother Veniamin, was a statistical and ethnographic survey of the Central Black Earth region of Russia, which appeared as the second book of an eleven-volume series on Russia's principal geographic regions. She did the ethnographic portions, while her brother (editor of the series) compiled the statistics.[13] Semyonova also collected Russian folk costumes, and eventually with her friend Varvara Shneider acquired 1,465 items, subsequently donated to the Russian Ethnographic Museum.[14] Finally, Semyonova was an accomplished water-colorist. She received formal training in the 1880s at the School of the Society for the Encouragement of the Arts in St. Petersburg and continued to paint throughout her life. Some of her works now hang in Russian state institutions and galleries.[15] Her interest in painting was to become an asset in her investigation of

12. Information on Semyonova's life comes chiefly from the previously cited eulogy by Varvara Shneider published in *Izvestiia imp. Russkogo geograficheskogo obshchestva*, vol. 43 (1907), 41-62. A portion of Semyonova's study of songs was published in the journal *Zhivaia Starina* under the title "Pesni Riazanskoi gubernii," 4:2, otd. 2. Two other of her works appearing in the same journal are "Prazdniki (Riazanskoi gub. Dankovskogo u.)," 1:4, otd. 5; and "Smert' i dusha v pover'iakh i rasskazakh krest'ian i meshchan Riazanskogo, Ranenburgskogo i Dankovskogo uezdov Riazanskoi gubernii," 8:2, otd. 2.

13. *Rossiia. Polnoe geograficheskoe opisanie nashego otechestva*, vol. 2: *Srednerusskaia chernozemnaia oblast'* (St. Petersburg, 1902).

14. The collection is mentioned in AGO, f. 58, op. 1, d. 36 (Kartoteka kollektsii, sobrannykh V. P. Shneider i O. P. Semenovoi Tian'-Shanskoi), l. 20. The bulk of the collection is now in Riazan province, and other portions are in Tambov and Orlov provinces.

Personal correspondence of Semyonova in regard to the costume collection can be found in Arkhiv AN SSSR, f. 906, op. 1, d. 26, ll. 213-14 and elsewhere.

15. At least one of her paintings is in the Riazan Art Gallery, a gift from her brothers Veniamin and Andrei. Others are in the Russian Museum in St. Petersburg, and I saw two hanging in the Geographic Society building in St. Petersburg. On the Riazan gallery and her schooling, see Riazanskii oblastnoi khudozhestvennyi muzei, *Russkoe iskusstvo 19–nachalo 20 v. Katalog* (Leningrad, 1982), 219. I am indebted to Olga Melnikova for this reference.

village life, for she confessed that many times while working at her easel, she was able to eavesdrop on peasant conversations.

This stratagem employed by Semyonova for overhearing conversations reveals her awareness of her status as an outsider in the village and her ability to devise means of getting at intimate details. She clearly sensed the otherness of the peasant world and regarded the peasants as different from educated, urbanized Russians in fundamental ways. She constituted her own identity as a person of Western scientific culture in opposition to the peasants she studied. For example, according to her, the boundary between childhood and adulthood, so clearly demarcated in educated society, collapsed in village society. Peasant children saw the world very much as did the adults. But instead of viewing this difference through the prism of the elite's paternalist ideology (which held that the childlike innocence of adult peasants required that they be guided and protected by the landlords), Semyonova stressed another aspect: the early exposure of children to the difficulties and cynicism of adult life. Peasant views of work, morality, and property were likewise quite different from her own, not to mention the treatment of women, whose lot as the brutalized work horses and chief preservers of social bonds in the family and community Semyonova portrays with a vividness achieved in no other study of Russian peasant life.

Since the ethnographer and the peasants shared formal membership in the Eastern Orthodox church, this fundamental social institution and their common faith might conceivably have united them. But here again a divide is evident. Semyonova devotes relatively little space to religion, but it is clear that she did not regard the peasants as Orthodox Christians. She depicts them as confused about questions of ultimate truth and salvation, even on their deathbeds. She tells of old people who in their last hours still wondered whether some dissident religious sects might not provide a better guide to heaven than their own official church. God was a physical reality for peasants, for he constituted a tangible presence, who brought rain or drought, health or illness. In this sense, God was more real than the tsar, who for most Russian villagers was a distant, unreachable figure. But the world of the peasant was populated as well by a wide range of creatures unknown to the Christian church, including powerful water, tree, house, and steambath sprites, and the most mighty and encompassing of all, Moist Mother Earth. We will see in Semyonova's study examples of people not only placing their hands on a Bible but also eating earth to seal an unbreakable pledge.

Here it is worth pointing out that one of the central issues in the scholarship on Russian religion is the question of syncretism (or *dvoeverie,* as it is known in Russian), the commingling of elements of local folk belief and the larger structure of Christian doctrine, the "little tradition" and "great tradition," as the two are labeled in the writings of the anthropologist Robert Redfield. The notion should be familiar in a culture such as ours that celebrates Christ's birth with the visit of an elf from the North Pole and the Resurrection with an oversize rabbit carrying baskets of eggs.[16] In the Russian village, the two traditions merge. Midwives and folk healers in their spells and prayers simultaneously invoke the assistance of Christian saints and nature spirits. Priests perform cleansing rituals to remove "unclean" forces of pre-Christian belief systems. Semyonova describes a scene in which a priest ritually cleanses a tub of pickled apples polluted by a dead mouse. Although her urban, scientific worldview led her to interpret this as a fraud committed by the priest in order to obtain a fee, the priest may well have understood what he was doing as a "Christian" service and not at all in conflict with his religious training.

One important aspect of village life that Semyonova does little to illuminate is kinship, even though conversations she reports by peasants about decision making in the village indicate the prominence of kin ties in local power relations. In this respect, Semyonova treats her subject quite differently than did leading

16. A point made by Donald W. Treadgold, "The Peasant and Religion," in *The Peasant in Nineteenth-Century Russia,* ed. Wayne S. Vucinich (Stanford: Stanford University Press, 1968), 72-107, in which he also develops Redfield's notions of the two traditions.

British and French anthropologists in later years; they placed kinship structure at the center of their analysis and deployed it as the principal comparative element, around which they then built their interpretation of the culture as a whole. We do see some of the workings of kinship relations in Semyonova's descriptions of weddings, christenings, and the like, but she never analyzes them directly or looks for them in specific stories. Possibly, this particular blind spot was a consequence of the similarity in kinship structures of peasant and urban Russian society. The focus on the otherness of an ethnographic subject may make it difficult for the researcher to see the similarities—or at least to rate them as instructive or significant.

It is also important to keep in mind that Semyonova was working before the time that kinship became a central focus in Western anthropology. The Russian ethnographic tradition within which she operated had until the twentieth century primarily a literary rather than an analytical orientation. Literature and literary criticism were the favored vehicles of social commentary in Russia from the mid-eighteenth to the early twentieth centuries, and the story of the people naturally was shaped by the powerful literary currents in society, first into a pseudo-classicist idyll of happy villagers dancing through fields of flowers in clean costumes, and later, under the influence of Romanticism and sentimentalism, into a vehicle for either the Official Nationality doctrine of the state, which extolled the greatness and uniqueness of the people, or the critical nativist stance of Slavophilism, which condemned the oppression of the people by the westernizing state bureaucracy. According to the great nineteenth-century historian of Russian ethnography A. N. Pypin (himself a leading literary critic), after the shift in political loyalties in the 1860s (when the Slavophiles turned statist and imperialistic), the Russian and Ukrainian ethnographic movements again aligned with the current literary movements, in some cases with the westernizing and in others with the nativist-imperialist.[17] Because Russian ethnog-

17. A. N. Pypin, *Istoriia russkoi etnografii*, 4 vols (St. Petersburg, 1890-92).

raphers thought of themselves as writers of literature, the more analytical and quantitative approaches to the peasantry were produced by other researchers, such as statisticians and medical writers. Semyonova clearly belonged to the established ethnographic tradition and saw herself as a creative but objective writer who used words to describe peasant life much as she used water colors to render village scenes and landscapes.

Might Semyonova possibly have felt a bond with the female peasants in their common subjection to the patriarchal authority that permeated Russian society from top to bottom? Semyonova's own father was said to have been an emotionally distant, patriarchal figure.[18] She describes with intensity the brutality with which men enforced their power in the village. But she also notes cases of women who beat their husbands and, more commonly, women who refused to take extra employment even when their husbands had contracted for them to do the work. Most important, her descriptions reveal the ideology and reality of patriarchal power as compromised in several key areas of peasant life. Decisions on whether babies were to live or die were left entirely to women, ensuring their control over family limitation. Decisions about when and whom to marry were also primarily left to women, who thus gained the power to build and shape kin ties, which, as Semyonova points out in another context, were central to village politics. The descriptions of property and the responsibilities of spouses likewise reveal the limits of husbands' authority to use their wives' goods or coerce them to perform certain tasks.

Semyonova depicts these cases of female control effectively, but she seems unaware of their subversive impact. Of course, Pierre Bourdieu was not available to instruct her in the creative disjunction between ideology and practice.[19] Contemporary readers should also not forget that Russian patriarchal authority (like any enduring system of dominance) owed much of its success to

18. See portrayal by W. Bruce Lincoln, *Petr Petrovich Semenov-Tian-Shanskii: The Life of a Russian Geographer* (Newtonville, Mass.: Oriental Research Partners, 1980).
19. See his *Outline of a Theory of Practice* (Cambridge: Cambridge University Press, 1977), especially chapter 4.

just such surrenders of power. By yielding these spaces to women, men also yielded responsibility for risky decisions (risky in relation to both this life and the next) and preserved for themselves a moral high ground from which they could pass judgment on their wives' decisions. Not surprisingly, Semyonova does not work at this level of abstraction; nor is she able to transcend the language and attitudes of her day. She sympathizes with the women she observes, but she uses the categories of thought and expression of the time to describe the behavior of her villagers.

Is it possible that Semyonova's descriptions of peasant women reflect some of her feelings in regard to her own troubled life with men, the dominance of her famous father, the tragedy of her love affair? Men are not portrayed very attractively in her work. With a few exceptions, she depicts them as violent toward women, unconcerned about their children, and satisfied to stand around while women do heavy work. When she explores the affective life of the peasant, whether Ivan was capable of expressing love for his sweetheart or his wife, the findings are not especially encouraging. The primary expression of love, if we are to believe the reports of married peasant women, are the willingness of some husbands to perform needed farm work at their wives' request and to forbear beating them. Semyonova tells the story of one such man, Petrukha, whose wife was envied by all the other women of the village. He hurried to do whatever his wife directed (even if he had to hide or explain away his submissiveness to his male friends). But Semyonova also adds: "Unfortunately, men such as Petrukha and the type of relationship he has with his wife are rare indeed. To tell the truth, this is the only case I know of."

The story of the submissive husband is just one of a number of descriptions of actual villagers that were included in the published text of Semyonova's work, to which I have added several others that I found in her archives. It is these stories of real people rather than her composite "Ivan" and his family that make the study especially vivid and valuable. Her composite descriptions usually show the peasants as brutal, selfish, and unfriendly, whereas her vignettes about actual people give us a more nuanced portrayal, including a glimpse of the peasants' admirable qualities and the regard they could show for one another.

Many things about the peasants nevertheless seemed to perplex and even anger Semyonova. Despite her genuine interest in and concern for them, she remained fixed in her own cultural frame. Her stance was that of a progressive, westernizing member of the Russian intelligentsia. She wanted the peasants to share her respect for private property, her values of thrift and hard work, and she believed that without these values they could not become enlightened and productive citizens of a modern society. Yet she recognized that her values might seem useless to the peasants, given the social and economic constraints under which they lived. And she was able to grasp and convey some of their deeply felt grievances. She sensed their contempt for the enfeebled landlord class (which was passing from the scene, unable for the most part to compete, and selling out its property to merchants and wealthy peasants). She also saw the peasants' powerful desire to wrest from the landlords the land that they felt was rightfully theirs—and their equally strong urge to hide from people like her the knowledge of that impulse. While able to glimpse such peasant attitudes, she was unable to enter the peasants' mental world. Instead, she remained mystified and annoyed that they rejected her values, did not respect private property, stole from landlords, and assaulted their better-off neighbors.

The work of modern anthropologists may be of help in making sense of the views Semyonova describes. Peasants often seem to think of the world (or at least their world of the village) as constrained by a "limited good," that is, a space containing only a fixed amount of all goods worth having, including land, wealth, respect, and friendship. The idea of an expanding economy, an enlarging pie that will bring more benefits to everyone, is alien, or at least was so until recent technological breakthroughs. This way of seeing things may have arisen out of the circumstances of a fixed land base and low technology that constrained the growth of productivity in peasant societies before the twentieth century.[20] If "Ivan" was able to purchase more land and put more food on his table, it was food taken out of the mouths of the rest of the community. In this view, the assaults on and robberies of a better-off peasant's orchard, to select an example used by Semyonova, were efforts to get back a (wrongful) private appropriation of a community good.

Semyonova laments the peasants' habit of immediately spending any money that came their way and of spending their last kopeck on weddings and harvest festivals. Yet from the point of view of "limited good," these expenditures make sense. If private accumulation of wealth was understood as a form of robbery, it would naturally have engendered resentment. Large outlays for weddings and parties served as a form of redistribution and at the same time allowed the donor to acquire "symbolic capital," respect and status, personal leverage. Chapter 10 contains a story about a peasant who returned to the village after many years of work in town and won a share of the family property in a lawsuit against his brother. He then threw a big party for the community. His hosting of the other villagers would be labeled by us (as by Semyonova) as a bribe to ensure the community's ratification of the decision of the township court. Yet the villagers may have seen the man's behavior as a proper reallocation of some of the goods he had acquired through the lawsuit, and they would then have understood their ratification of the court's decision as justified by virtue of his good-neighborliness.

Semyonova tells in chapter 7 of the ridicule with which peasants greeted one of their fellows who thought too highly of himself, a story that reveals how even a good such as respect cannot be freely appropriated. She describes how the man, on

20. I am relying here on the work of Edward C. Banfield, *The Moral Basis of a Backward Society* (New York: The Free Press, 1958), and George M. Foster, "Peasant Society and the Image of the Limited Good," *American Anthropologist*, vol. 67 (1965), 293-315. See also the symposium on this topic with contributions by Foster, Oscar Lewis, and Julian Pitt-Rivers in *Human Organization* (Winter 1960-61), 174-84. I want to thank Steven L. Hoch for directing me to this literature.

approaching the other male peasants, was "met with shrieks of laughter," for peasants do not like "uppityness" and an air of self-importance. The ridicule is evidently aimed at restoring a balance in status allocation among the peasant men. One who takes too much respect for himself, in view of the "limited good" notions of the peasant mental world, is robbing from the others and needs to be reduced to the general level.

By the same token, villagers had to be concerned about attacks on their character. Where material goods are scarce, the symbolic capital of personal honor plays a large role in ensuring a person's ability to participate fully in community affairs, make contracts, be listened to. We see how the question of personal reputation affected women in Semyonova's report on a court case brought by a woman who was accused of being a "slut." She demanded and received retribution from her false accuser, whom the court sent to jail for this crime.

To sum up, even though Semyonova renders marvelously detailed and striking portrayals of peasant behavior, she makes little effort to enter the peasants' cultural frame. She remains outside and is entirely confident of her superiority to the peasants. Unlike some populist writers who extolled the wisdom of the folk, she is not inclined to celebrate or to romanticize them. Clearly, a central purpose of her study is to counter naive views of the peasants as naturally cooperative, communitarian beings who will provide the foundation for a new order of social peace and harmony. She hoped that a more realistic understanding of the peasants would facilitate their transformation into a modern educated citizenry.

Semyonova's friends wrote about her "love for the people," a remark that I found puzzling because it is usually associated with populist thinkers who idealized villagers. Love is not the emotion that dominates her study, marked as it is by anger and condescension as well as understanding and sympathy. In my conversations with her relatives, I asked about this puzzle, noting that "the picture she paints of peasant life is done in very dark colors." Anastasia Mikhailovna brusquely responded: "Regrettably, such was their life." When I then inquired how Semyonova expressed her love for the people, I was told that she worked with them to improve their lives. Among other things, she established a school for peasant girls in which they learned craft work in addition to general education, and she helped the villagers to organize means for preventing and fighting fires.

Finally, one clue to Semyonova's sometimes bleak view of peasant life might be found in her own experience as revealed in her autobiographical notes, a few of which were published in the introduction to the Russian edition of this study. They are dreamy and sad, much concerned with mortality and immortality. "I have long been troubled," she writes, "by my desire to give a part of me to other people. This desire sometimes reaches a glowing heat, but then, oh so often, I get to thinking about my insignificance, the complete emptiness of my existence, and it gives me pause. What does it matter that from time to time there comes this bright, burning sensation, when next to it, I feel the dreary, heavy burden of my long years of useless existence? True, fate has shaken me rather roughly, but what of those who have suffered even worse grief and not sat with hands tied? But I merely sat and cried, wept through all the best part of my life, day after day dulling in me the awareness that you only live once, and that unused powers do not become invigorated or revitalized as years go on, that the sun does not stand still if toward evening you take up some lengthy labor." And in reference to her decision to write, she continues: "All this is associated with me personally. But life threw me together with many people; many of them have already gone, never to return, and others will gradually depart as well. . . . And so I want to imprint, if only dimly, their dear shadows on paper. Perhaps, sometime in the future, passing by chance through someone's vivid consciousness, my pale images will blaze forth and spring to life for at least an instant. For the sake of this 'perhaps,' for this small deferral of oblivion and the impenetrable shadow, I have decided to take up the pen." Semyonova's inclination to see her own life as sad, a series of personal losses, isolation, and weeping, may have caused her to think of life in general as unhappy and therefore to miss seeing the moments of joy and contentment that her peasants undoubtedly experienced. In viewing the life of this community, we can see only what Semyonova was willing to see for herself, and in the way she was able to see it.

I have found little more about the elusive person through whose lens we view her peasant community. She led a secluded life among a small circle of friends, but she managed nevertheless to produce a priceless record of peasant life, a record that offers us insight into the lives and attitudes of Russian villagers on the eve of a revolution that would demand their participation in the building of a modern socialist state.

—D.L.R.

Village Life

in Late Tsarist Russia

1

❖❖❖

IVAN'S PARENTS

Semyonova begins her story with a description of the peasant Ivan's parents at the time they married and began their family. By contrasting the customs at that time (about 1863) with the time of her observations of Ivan the adult (about 1900), she is able to illustrate the rapid changes that were taking place in Russian peasant society in the late nineteenth century.

❖

IVAN'S PARENTS were known as Stepan and Akulina. Stepan, a peasant of average means, was born under serfdom. Ivan was his third son and was born a year or two after the emancipation of privately owned peasants in 1861. Stepan and Akulina's livestock at the time of Ivan's birth included three horses (one of which was a yearling), fifteen sheep, one cow, a heifer, and a pig. Their hut, which was wooden, had three windows and an enclosed entryway (*sentsa*). Nearby were a workyard, a small granary, and a threshing barn.

Farm tools included two wagons, two wooden, wheelless plows, one harrow, two types of harnesses, two scythes, two rolls of sackcloth (*veret'ia*), a sleigh, an ax, two spades, and two flails.

Household utensils consisted of a cabbage cleaver, four cast-

Peasant married couple hauling goods in a cart. Village of Murmino in Riazan district. Courtesy of the Riazan Museum.

iron kettles, seven tubs, two buckets, a ladle (*korets*), a churn, six earthenware pots, four dishes, a trough, a lamp, one size-four bottle, a scutch (for flax and hemp), two spinning wheels, two hackles with boards (*dontsa*) to brace them, two hand grinders, one table, two regular benches, a sleeping bench and a counter, a washtub, oven prongs (which are called a "stag" [*rogach*] because of their resemblance to antlers), a loom, three frying pans, two rakes, a sifter, and two sieves.

The young married couple harvested eighteen shocks of rye from their $6\frac{3}{4}$ acres of land, or about twenty-six hundred pounds of rye. In addition, they produced about six hundred pounds of millet (*proso*), thirty-five hundred pounds of potatoes, and eight shocks of oats.

When Stepan and Akulina married, Akulina's family had to provide a trousseau. In those days, a dowry of money was never used. It was customary to supply the bride with clothing: linen cloths (from five to twenty pieces about twenty-five yards each), two to five checked skirts, four to six shirts, one or two cotton sarafans, bedding (a feather pillow, a thick unquilted coverlet, i.e., a blanket). Other types of women's household goods were accepted, such as a spinning wheel or a hand grinder—although in general the dowry was a minor consideration. The groom's family focused mainly on the physical characteristics (health) and aptitude for work (abilities) of the prospective wife.

The groom would give his bride-to-be a brideprice, which consisted of about ten or fifteen rubles, a sheepskin coat, a light coat made from coarse peasant cloth, fur slippers, felt boots, between 75 and 150 pounds of flour, a measure of groats, and several gallons of vodka.[1]

Nowadays linen cloths are no longer included in the dowry. As the people explain, "The flax crops have been poor in recent years," and brides "are not the good spinners they were in the old days." Instead people focus mainly on whether the bride is well dressed, whether she has woolen sarafans, a shawl, shoes, a coat made from fine cloth, and the like. (In some villages, shifts and woolen skirts of the old type are going out of style and being replaced by sarafans. In these villages, women's everyday apparel consists of skirts, stockings, tight-fitting long-waisted jackets, sheepskin coats, and shirts made from homespun cotton; the rest of their clothes are made from manufactured cloth.)[2] Villagers demand just as many shirts for the trousseau now as they did previously, and the bedding is better than it used to be: two pillows, one made with feathers, the other with cotton wadding; two blankets, one an unquilted coverlet filled with wadding and

1. Although Semyonova writes that the brideprice was given to the bride, it would normally go to the father of the bride (or the head of her household, if it was not her father) in compensation for her lost services.
2. The parenthetical material comes from a much later point in the published study, where it appeared unconnected to surrounding material. In inserting it here, I deleted from the original paragraph an inconsistency: Semyonova had noted baldly that "woolen skirts are not worn anymore," without the qualifier "in some villages."

one a quilted cotton blanket. The groom's family gives less and less for the brideprice. Sometimes only one fur coat, sometimes only about seven rubles—and that is all.

In recent times, a money dowry has been given to the groom (about five to ten rubles), especially if his betrothed is known to have some failing, such as being hard of hearing or cross-eyed, or being "oldish" (i.e., considerably older than the groom), or if a rumor has spread that she has been "fooling around."

When Stepan and Akulina married about thirty years ago, the average age of marriage was sixteen to nineteen years for girls, eighteen to twenty for boys. In relatively rare exceptions, a family might ask the bishop for permission to marry a boy not quite eighteen years of age.[3] Even more rarely were fifteen-year-old girls given in marriage. Although it was considered dangerous for a girl to stay unmarried until she was twenty (because eligible bachelors would start to pass her by), a girl's family viewed her as a source of labor and consequently valued her, and they were not in a hurry to get rid of her. Yet they were eager to marry off a boy young and thereby obtain his wife as an additional worker for the family. As a result, marriage between an eighteen-year-old male and an eighteen-to-twenty-year-old female is not uncommon even today. There are still cases of seventeen-year-old boys marrying. Every married woman eagerly awaits the opportunity to be relieved in her work by a young daughter-in-law. [Mothers express this wish in the lullabies they sing to their infants.]

> I'm rocking my son
> I hope for a better life for myself.
> I'm rocking my daughter
> For her, I hope but for a kind household.[4]

About fifteen or twenty years ago, a man with a mustache and

3. The civil law set the minimum age for marriage at eighteen for males and sixteen for females. Ecclesiastical officials were nevertheless permitted to lower the age by six months in individual cases.

4. That is to say, in-laws who will welcome her as a guest and not treat her as a slave. [Semyonova]

beard was considered old. A girl who married such a man would be a laughingstock. Of course, people also made fun of a man who married a spinster. Women over twenty frequently married widowers, although in general it was considered more suitable for widowers to marry widows. Such weddings took place very simply; they were small family affairs without much merrymaking and were jokingly referred to as "cuckoo's weddings" (a widow is known as a "bitter cuckoo"). People would say, "Our widower is taking in a housekeeper for the work season."

Now women marry in the age range of sixteen to twenty-five, and men from age eighteen to twenty-seven. More commonly, women marry in the seventeen to twenty-two age range, and only rarely at sixteen and at twenty-three to twenty-five. Men very often marry only after completing their military service.

It is also considered no disgrace for a widower to marry a girl "with a past," as we say.

2

❖❖❖

CHILDBIRTH, CHRISTENING, WIFE BEATING

This chapter begins with the grim subject of infant death. It was an everyday occurrence in Russian villages at the time Semyonova was writing. Nearly half of Russian babies failed to survive to age five, an infant mortality rate among the highest ever recorded anywhere. Most of these deaths were caused by diarrhea and respiratory illnesses, but the lying-over deaths that Semyonova reports here also made an important contribution. These were deaths caused by mothers who, presumably in their sleep, rolled over on and smothered the babies they had placed in bed with them during the night for convenience in breastfeeding. In Europe generally at the time of rising fertility in the eighteenth century, these lying-over deaths became epidemic, so much so that it is difficult to believe that they were wholly accidental. Although Semyonova seems to say here that the deaths were accidental, at another point in her notes she asserts that some babies were purposely killed in this way (see below, p. 98). At this time, Russian villages were experiencing very high fertility, and youthful clumsiness alone seems an inadequate explanation of why more than half the mothers were lying over their infants.[1] *More likely, the women were asserting*

1. Sweden had particularly high rates of over-lying in the eighteenth century, and the priests there seemed to realize that women were limiting the population in this way—even if the rather obtuse historian of the practice refused to accept the priests' insight. A. Thompson, *Barnkvävningen* (Uppsala, 1960).

control, with the limited means at their command, over a chaotic and dangerous population growth. We will see other examples of their efforts at control later.

The third and fourth paragraphs of the chapter contain a description (found among Semyonova's notes) of an actual couple, Vasilii and Akulina, on whom the composite picture that follows of "Ivan's" parents, Stepan and Akulina, is based. (I use the name "Stepan" throughout, however.)[2] *It is interesting to see how closely the composite fit the real case, and also to observe the more natural feeling Semyonova has for the actual Akulina. Farther on, I include another paragraph from Semyonova's field notes about the calling of the midwife, again to show its role in the building of the composite picture. In both representations, emphasis on the intervention of the birthing mother's natal family at a time of personal crisis underlines the continuing deep affective bonds among these women, in contrast to the practical, and sometimes exploitative, relationship of the husband's family to the young wife.*

❖

YOUNG PEOPLE at the time of marriage frequently are not fully mature in their physical development. There is a saying that "the young start developing from the time of the wedding," i.e., they are still maturing after their wedding. As a consequence, the first two to three children are born weak and usually do not survive. Sometimes this is also a result of the total lack of experience on the part of the young mother in caring for a baby. Moreover, young mothers very often smother their children accidentally in their

2. At another point in her notes, Semyonova refers to Ivan's parents as Stepan and Lukeria (see pages 119-20 of the published research program in *Zapiski RGO*). It is not clear which of these four names, if any, belonged to the couple on which the composite picture was built.

sleep. The mother sometimes places her infant between herself and her husband to give the baby her breast, goes to sleep, rolls over on the baby, and smothers it. A good half of the women have overlain at least one child in this way—they do it most often in their young years when they sleep soundly. For overlying a child, the priest imposes a penance.

When Akulina married Stepan and joined his family, Stepan's parents were still fairly young, the father forty and the mother forty-two years of age. Stepan also had a brother who was around sixteen, a thirteen-year-old sister, and another brother two years old.

[Here begins the description of the actual couple.]

At first, Stepan and Akulina were rather shy toward one another. Stepan's mother bossed Akulina around. The first child, a weak, emaciated girl, was born a year and a half after the wedding. The young mother did not know how to care for her, and the baby girl died after a few weeks. After her death, Akulina was still in the process of growing up and filling out. Soon she became fairly rosy-cheeked and plump. A year after the death of her first child, she gave birth to a second, and two years after that a third one arrived. Both were boys. The second one died from diarrhea by the time his mother became pregnant again, this time with a third son (Ivan). This third son was born right in the middle of the summer field-work season.

The family of Stepan and Akulina looked forward to the first child. Stepan's father even joked that "my daughter-in-law is going to provide me with a grandson." But when a girl was born, the grandparents stopped thinking about her as soon as she was baptized. They did not even express any sorrow about her death. The young father, too, did not feel much regret over it. When the second child was expected, no one said anything about it. But they all were happy when they saw that a boy was born. In contrast, when the second boy came along, the father paid almost no attention to it, and when the third child (Ivan) was expected, even Akulina herself was distressed. "There's just going to be too many kids," she complained. She lost weight, because at the time she was still nursing her second son. Dark spots appeared on her face, and she aged so rapidly that no one would have guessed that she was only twenty-two years old. It was with a feeling of relief that she buried her second son, who died of diarrhea at the time of the St. Peter's fast in June.[3]

[The composite picture resumes.]

[The attitudes of parents toward the birth of children vary according to sex and birth order.] The first child is awaited with a certain degree of excitement. Sometimes the husband will tease his wife: "You just might bring *me* a son, mother." She might reply: "Whomever God wills, I might even have the good sense to bear a daughter for myself." (A daughter is a help to her mother, a nursemaid to the children.) The husband's mother announces to the neighbors with satisfaction that "our young one is certainly putting on weight." They all discuss whom to ask to be godparents. The father, naturally, expects a son. There is even a saying: "A son is for the father, a daughter for the mother." A mother is not much concerned about the sex of her first child. A father will, however, behave with complete indifference toward a daughter, as well as toward a second and third son. Mothers usually begin to feel burdened by the third child. A father may express his satisfaction with the birth of his first son, reporting to his neighbors: "My Aniutka after all brought me a son." Or when inviting someone to be godfather: "My wife did not let me down; she delivered a son." Yet in the family they say [more crudely]: "Our gal dropped a boy."[4] A mother, when cuddling and kissing the child, may be told by those present to "rejoice in your first-born!" A mother commonly uses pet words in addressing her child, such as "my little sonny (or girlie), my beauty, my golden darling, my berry, my dear little baby."

If the first child is a girl, the feeling in the family is mostly one of disappointment. One of the women might remark: "Oh well, at least she can be a nursemaid." By the following day, no one gives a thought to the baby girl. The friends and acquaintances of a man whose first-born is a girl, and in general the other men in the

3. These two paragraphs can be found on p. 135 of the published text.
4. The verb used here, *rasprastalas'*, refers to births by animals.

village, have the right to beat the young father when he appears at work. "Why did you have a daughter?" they say. They often thrash him soundly, and he has to keep quiet about it, for this is a well-established custom.

If a woman happens to give birth often, members of the family naturally respond disapprovingly. They do not hesitate to make crude remarks in this regard: "Ugh, you fertile thing, you surround yourself with children like a rabbit. Better that your puppies died off. Here you are with a litter every year; look here, the bitch has a litter again," and the like. These remarks often come from a woman's mother-in-law.[5]

During pregnancy, a woman continues to be responsible for all her usual chores, both in the household and in the field—including binding the sheaves, weeding, threshing, gathering in the hemp, planting and digging potatoes—right up to the onset of labor. Women frequently give birth while performing a domestic chore, such as kneading bread, or even when they are at work in the field; others do so riding in a bumpy wagon as they are hurrying home after being prompted by the first pangs of the approaching birth. Some women, when they feel labor pains, run toward home "like a newborn lamb," as it is said. When the pains increase, they lie down on the ground, and then they run again when the pains subside, yelling at the top of their lungs, "like a helpless trembling lamb."

At the onset of labor pains, the midwife sometimes tries to drag the laboring mother into the stove and steam her there in order to speed up the childbirth.[6] It is the job of the mother-in-law to fetch

5. Again, we see Semyonova's representation of the mother-in-law as having less an affective bond than a controlling and disciplining relationship with the daughters-in-law residing in her home and over whom she exercises authority. This is such a cliché in accounts of peasant life that one wonders if Semyonova is drawing as much on the stereotype as on her own observations, but it is true that the female labor hierarchy of the household was similar to that of an artisan shop, in which the mother-in-law acted as the master and the younger women as workers and apprentices.

6. Yes, *into* the stove. The large Russian stove, which takes up from a quarter to a third of the main room of the house, often has a deep side opening large enough to accommodate a human body.

the midwife. She tries to haggle a bit with the midwife about the usual fee. The customary payment for the delivery of a baby, or "receiving," as the peasants say, would be a loaf of rye bread, plus another bread made of sifted flour and called "pirog," a cotton shawl worth twenty kopecks, and ten kopecks in cash. If the midwife living nearby does not want to agree to such an unprofitable arrangement, the mother-in-law will go to another village or to the far end of her own village to summon another midwife, a woman from her own kin who charges a smaller fee. Frequently, at this time, the young, inexperienced mother is left in pain completely unattended. It is a good thing for her if her mother or sister lives in the vicinity. They can step in and will not begrudge the midwife her usual fee in kind. And so the midwife appears. When summoning the midwife, women usually avoid direct reference to the birth, so that no one except the midwife will know that the labor pains have begun. This secrecy is believed to make things easier for the laboring mother. So they say something like: "What's this, old woman, you promised to look at my cow and you aren't coming?"[7]

[Here begins the description of the real Akulina.]

On the eve of the birth of Akulina's third son, Ivan, Akulina had been weeding a field of millet. After returning to the field the following morning, she felt the initial labor pains. At first she thought that the work had given her a severe backache. Her mother-in-law went to get a village midwife (*babka*). The women she approached were reluctant to come, however, because the stinginess of Akulina's mother-in-law was well known. They haggled over the price. The mother-in-law wanted to pay them only "a pie," which meant wheat bread made from sifted flour. (A midwife is normally offered one loaf of rye bread, one loaf of wheat bread, a cotton kerchief, and ten kopecks.) The women did not agree, and Akulina's mother-in-law said she would go to

7. When I was doing ethnographic field work in 1990, interviewing peasant women in Leningrad, Novgorod, and Moscow provinces, I found this belief still very much alive among women of central Russian villages who gave birth in the 1930s and 1940s.

another village instead. During this time, Akulina lay without any assistance. Finally, Akulina's own mother intervened and promised to give a midwife wheat bread. The midwife arrived at the home not long before Akulina gave birth.

[The composite picture resumes.]

[At the home of the birthing mother,] the midwife prays for a timely birth. She fills her mouth with water and then empties it onto her hands, which she soaps if there is soap in the house. She inspects or, as they say, "witnesses" the laboring mother. If the birth is progressing slowly, the mother is led around the table three times. Or the midwife calls in the husband and makes him pass three times between the legs of the standing woman. If this does not help, and especially if the labor drags on more than twenty-four hours, they hold a mass in the church and open the Tsar's gates in the iconostasis.[8] To speed up the birth, the woman grasps a rafter in the hut (which is called "hanging by the beam"). If the rafters are too high up, then two woven bands are attached to them, and the birthing mother holds on to these. By the time of the delivery, the bands have stretched out far enough to allow the woman to kneel on the floor. Sometimes she has to hang so long from the beams that her arms hurt for two weeks after the birth. But it also happens that the baby is born just as the mother is being hung from the beams.

When the baby is not coming out "the right way," i.e., it is coming out feet first or crooked, the midwife drops the mother down a makeshift slide. One end of a wide board is placed against the wall and fastened down at an angle. With the help of the husband, the midwife places the woman on her back, head down, near the top of the board. Then the husband and the midwife let go of her, and she slides quickly headfirst while the husband and the midwife see to it that she does not fall sideways. This rapid motion

8. The iconostasis or icon wall is a principal element in the architecture of Eastern Orthodox churches, a high wall or screen in front of the altar on which are mounted tiers of icons in a specific hierarchy. In the center of the iconostasis is a double door leading to the altar known variously as the "Tsar's gates," the "holy gates," or the "majestic gates."

and some additional shaking are thought to straighten out the child, so that on the second try it can come out properly, i.e., headfirst. When the child is born, the midwife ties off its umbilical cord with flax or thread. If the placenta does not come out for a long time, the mother's braids are shoved into her mouth (if the braids are too short, fingers are used) so that she will choke and thus supposedly facilitate the rapid expulsion of the placenta.[9] When the placenta is out, the midwife bathes the newborn and washes the mother. Occasionally she will use this opportunity to "straighten out" the head of the newborn, working it with her hands to give it a rounded shape. If the nose seems too flat, it, too, will be corrected.

If the baby is born barely alive, the practice is to blow three times on the top of its head, between its shoulder blades, and on the soles of its feet. Other steps include slapping the baby on its rear end and administering artificial respiration as if to a drowned man.

In rich families, the midwife sometimes stays on for three or four days after the birth, eating at their table. The baby of poor peasants, however, is left entirely to its mother's care from the first day.

Mothers who are concerned about neatness put straw into the cradle and change it every day or two. More often, though, the baby is placed into a dirty cradle lined with its mother's soiled old skirt: "He can just as well lie on the skirt, no better than anybody else. Others didn't seem to die; they survived." When the mother does not have enough milk or when the child is left alone, it is given a rag pacifier [known as a *soska*]. The mother, sister, or grandmother chews on potatoes, rye bread, or bagels, spits them out into a thin rag, ties it up with a thread, and the *soska* is ready.

9. According to a doctor in rural practice, women usually gave birth with their hair undone, an observation that fits with the notion Russian villagers had that doors, gates, trunk tops, and the like should be opened in order to ease and speed the birth process. K. I. Shidlovskii, "K kharakteristike russkoi narodnoi meditsiny," *Meditsinskii vestnik*, no. 3 (1884), 39.

Young mother holds her newborn swaddled in the Russian manner. Sapozhok district of Riazan province. Courtesy of the Riazan Museum.

Sometimes the same rag pacifier is used over and over again without washing and acquires a repulsive, sour odor.

By the third or fourth day after delivery, mothers get up and return to their household chores, sometimes even to the hard work, such as kneading dough and putting it into the oven. Occasionally, even on the day after the birth the new mother must light the stove herself. In such conditions, it takes a long time for the woman to recover, and the child is consequently neglected; it is left alone in a dirty cradle wearing a soaking-wet diaper, crying its heart out in hunger pains, and its navel swells and hurts (which the women refer to as "hernia"). The new mother naturally gets along the whole time on ordinary peasant food. Sometimes she expresses a desire to eat fresh cucumbers or apples, and the family may occasionally satisfy this whim. It should be noted that on such occasions the neighbors may turn out to be quite helpful and share with the mother some of their cucumbers or apples if she does not have a supply of her own. There was one case in which a mother in the village of Muraevnia (about a mile from the estate where this writer lived) died after eating too many of the cucumbers brought over by a neighbor on the second day after the birth.

A baby is usually baptized on the second or, less often, the third day after it is born. The names most often given are, for males, Ivan, Vasilii, Mikhail, and Aleksei, and for females, Maria, Anna, Avdotia, Akulina, and Tatiana. For the most part, the priest gives names at his own discretion. The priest is, however, more apt to ask a wealthy family than a poor one what name they want for their child. For a baptism the priest receives fifty kopecks, plus some rye bread. The rye bread comes from the mother, and the money is given by the godfather. The godmother gives the mother the cloth in which the child is wrapped after being dipped in the baptismal font, as well as about 1.5 yards of inexpensive cotton print and a blouse for the baby.

The christening ceremony, which usually occurs after a mass, is customarily followed by a "christening dinner" for the godparents. People like to go to the christening of a child from a rich family but are less interested in attending a christening in a poor family, because "the refreshments are meager." At the christening dinner, the parents serve vodka (the amount varies in accordance with their means), cucumbers with kvass, kasha, and a "pirog." In addition to these things, a rich family may offer cabbage soup, noodles, pancakes, and even chicken. At the dinner, the new father is served oversalted kasha and told: "This kasha will be as salty for you as it was salty for the mother to bring you a son (or daughter)."[10]

The christening normally takes place about eleven o'clock in the morning or twelve noon. After the ceremony, the parents [or grandparents] of the newborn invite the godparents to their house for the christening dinner, as well as the parents of the new mother, her sisters, and sometimes her brother. Vodka is served immediately. The average peasant provides, depending on the harvest, from one bottle up to five pints [a *chetvert'*] of vodka and even more, if he is the type that does not pass up an occasion to get drunk and, at the same time, happens to have extra money to spend on liquor. The hosts offer drinks first to the godparents, and only after that to the rest of the guests. When offering drinks, the hosts say, "Here's to the godchild!" The godparents reply, "Here's to the grandchild!" if the hosts are the grandparents of the baby, and "Here's to the son!" if the hosts are the parents of the newborn. Good wishes [in reference to the child's future] are not expressed.[11] Only the midwife, who stays with the hosts because her duties include helping with the christening dinner and picking up afterwards, may say to the godparents when she is serving the kasha: "Scoop up some kasha with your spoons and [come up with something] for your godchild." Guests place copper money and small silver coins on a plate as gifts for the new mother. Normally, only the godparents give money, though sometimes the

10. This custom, known to anthropologists as "couvade," binds the father to the birth process and the child by causing him to sense some of its unpleasantness.
11. Semyonova does not explain this laconic remark, perhaps because the reasons were obvious at the time. The great uncertainty of the survival of small children constrained projections about their future. And in the thinking of villagers, to anticipate a child's survival was likely to hasten its end.

maternal grandfather, in a fit of generosity, will also place a coin on the plate.

The midwife, while she is serving bread and cake, also places her saucer on the table; the guests fill it with a few two-kopeck silver pieces, and on rare occasions someone will drop in a five-kopeck piece. The guests stay at the table for two or three hours talking about their affairs, the harvesting, the crops, and the sowing, or they gossip about the neighbors. When the vodka is plentiful, everyone gets drunk. But songs are not sung, as this is not appropriate at a christening dinner. The new mother is also in attendance, but, because the christening usually takes place the day after the delivery, she stays removed from the crowd, resting on a bench in the back of the room. The newborn wails. The guests joke around. When the baby makes too much noise, they say [to the mother]: "Hey, you little cow, where did you hide your teats?" The sisters of the new mother sometimes leave the table and go over to the mother to redo the baby's swaddling clothes. When the guests leave, the father of the newborn, the grandparents, and the midwife show them to the door, bowing all the while.

When the midwife, having completed her responsibilities, leaves the house, the family gives her "a send-off." The new mother brings her a wash basin filled with water and with hops soaking in it. First the midwife washes her hands, and then the new mother washes hers and while doing so drops into the water ten kopecks as payment for the midwife. This ablution is performed "so as to alleviate the condition of the new mother." The ritual is also known as "silverplating the midwife." After this, the midwife is treated to vodka, receives the amount of bread and cake that is due her, and takes her leave.

The midwife's assistance is sometimes sought in treating a sick baby. Most often she is called on to treat "hernia"[12] and recurrent crying. For the treatment of hernia, the midwife mixes horse dung, strained through a cloth, with mother's milk and administers this potion to the infant. Crying is the result of the "evil eye," and the

12. A rupture of the umbilicus.

midwife exorcises it in three sessions—two at dusk, and one at dawn. For this she goes out into a field with the baby, faces the sun, and bowing to it says: "God bless us. The sunset, summer lightning, fair maid, evening, morning, day, night, midday, midnight, hour, minute! Take the crying from Ivan and give him sleep and health. Amen." The incantation is repeated three times. In return for this ceremony or for the treatment, the midwife receives payment in bread or grain. Diarrhea in children is treated with sacramental wine bought at the church for five kopecks and given to the sick child in drops.

Formerly, in the period of serfdom, mothers returned to the field three days after they gave birth, but the interval is now usually five to seven days. When the mother returns to field work, she either takes the child with her, or, if the field is not far from the house and she can run back to feed the baby, she leaves it with her older daughter or with an old woman. If the mother takes the baby into the field, she either places it, wrapped in rags, on a boundary strip, where a brother or sister five to seven years old will watch it, or, if she brings the cradle in the wagon, she places the baby in the cradle attached to the raised shaft of the wagon. Up to the age of one year, children are given something to chew on: the mother, the grandmother, or a sister chews a potato or a piece of bread and then transfers this "cud" with her fingers to the mouth of the child.

More often than not, the hard work that follows childbirth results in some degree of prolapse of the uterus. Sometimes such a fallen uterus can be very severe, but mild cases, in the opinion of the midwife, are nothing to be concerned about. Prolapsed uterus is not exceptional even among very young women, who experience it as a result of excessive work. The condition is treated with "kinderbalsam," known as "lifting drops." The midwife repairs the stomach by applying a clay pot to it. She places the woman on her back, rubs grease all over her stomach, and flips a pot over on it while quickly lighting a piece of yarn under the pot. This [vacuum] causes the stomach to be drawn into the pot. The smaller the pot, the better. The uterus is believed to be restored to its proper position, and the pain stopped, as a result of this treatment (called

Women gathering straw for storage in the large barn (*gumno*) at the rear. Photo by P. N. Semyonov from *Rossiia. Polnoe geograficheskoe opisanie,* vol. 2, p. 216.

"applying the pot," or "fixing the stomach"). Payment for this operation is again made in bread, a little flour, or groats. Another method is for the midwife to "steam" the new mother's abdomen by waving hot birch twigs just above it, and then to use her hands to push up on it several times so as to force the uterus into place.

The midwife employs still another method to "fix the stomach": she soaps her hands, forces the uterus into place, then pushes a peeled potato into the vagina and binds the lower abdomen tightly with a kerchief. A woman might go for a whole month to the midwife and have the operation repeated until she gets relief. Another manner of treating a prolapsed uterus is also in use. The midwife, with the help of the woman's husband, places the patient's head down and shakes her by the legs several times so as to "lift the stomach." After this the abdomen is bound. According to the midwives, all women experience this type of "stomach problem" at one time or another. One midwife claimed that some women develop extremely severe forms of fallen uterus because of their husbands' excessive drinking. "The fellow, when drunk, may lie on top of his wife all night long and not let her out from under him. The poor thing, she hurts and wants to cry from pain, but if she does, he will just beat her black and blue. She has no choice but to obey him, although after lying under a heavy, drunken man, her uterus is so badly displaced that she can neither stand nor sit." Many women told me that they suffered in this way, and despite this they are able to get pregnant and bear children.

[The last observations raise the question of violence of Russian men against their women.] As to the character and frequency of wife beating, it can be said that Stepan rarely beat Akulina when he was sober. But when he was drunk, he did so often and with whatever he could find. Observers note that drunks usually beat their wives when the women reproach them. A wife might, for example, accuse her drunken husband of "nuzzling the bottle again" or remark that "the stray dog has gorged himself again." The men will beat their wives out of jealousy. They beat them with sticks, oven prongs, boots, buckets, and whatever else is handy—or just slug or kick them. They drag them by their braids down the front steps so that their heads make a thumpity-thump noise. Not only the wife is beaten, but sometimes even the old father. In one village, a young fellow killed his father with a wagon shaft, beating him so hard that the father died from the blows. In the village of Muraevnia, there was a case of a drunken husband who killed his wife for infidelity. He rolled her braids around his hand and beat her head on the front steps, on the benches, and on the wall until she lapsed into a coma. She died a day later, never having regained consciousness.

If when beating his wife a husband breaks or damages one of the objects with which he has been meting out the punishment, he naturally is much more sorry about the loss of this tool than he is about his battered wife. The woman, too, grieves more over a broken oven fork than over her swollen side.

A young husband who finds out that his bride has not been chaste sometimes beats her cruelly on his wedding night, and this may serve as only a prelude to beatings that stretch out over the course of several months. The peasants consider it a man's duty to beat his wife if she, as they say, "brings home" another man's baby in the absence of her husband, something that occurs most often in the case of soldiers' wives.[13] If the husband is weak or sickly, unfit for work, then he usually catches it from the stronger party, his wife, who also reproaches him with words such as, "You good-for-nothing deadhead, I have to pull your weight."

A drunken husband sometimes beats his wife when she refuses to carry out some order of his, for example, to pull off his boots or put him to bed. She also catches it if she refuses to sleep with him. In a word, she is punished for any failure to fulfill her husband's wishes. I knew one peasant man who, when he was drunk, loved to abuse his wife in the following way: "Down, woman! On your knees! Put your head on the threshold. I am finally going to have my way and kill you!" The woman had to put her head down on the threshold without complaining, while he brandished an ax above her. This usually set the little children to crying and screaming. Then he would say: "If it were not for the children, you'd be dead by now," and he would let her go. If she did not obey him, he beat her cruelly, sometimes with a flail about the head. This is called "to wise up a wife" or "to heap scorn on a wife."

Another husband, when he was drunk, would get a few girls intoxicated and force them to sing a dance tune outside the window of his hut, while inside he forced his wife, under threat of a beating, to dance with him.

13. Peasant men who were unlucky enough to be drafted into the military had to serve for many years, leaving behind their wives and families. These husbandless women, fairly or unfairly, acquired as a group the reputation of "loose women." We will read more about them later in this study. For additional information, see Elise Kimerling, "Soldiers' Children, 1719–1856: A Study of Social Engineering in Imperial Russia," *Forschungen zur osteuropäischen Geschichte*, vol. 30 (Berlin, 1982), 74

3

❖❖❖

CHILDHOOD

After discussing basic child care, Semyonova enters into a discussion of the psychology of peasant youngsters. She sees their attitudes and behavior as conditioned by the promiscuous intimacy of peasant life. The precocious shrewdness of peasant children led her to the belief (so implausible to our modern way of thinking) that children saw the world in the same terms as adults. She also makes some comparisons of peasant children and "our children," that is, the children of educated urbanized people. While she no doubt idealized the conditions of children in educated families, her attitude reveals the chasm she sensed between the world of peasant family life and that of educated society.

Semyonova seems to have seen the roots of peasant morality in the values instilled in childhood, although she does not state this directly. Deceit to escape punishment was approved, as was the use of foul language or abuse of animals to vent frustration. Patriarchal authority was accepted implicitly; might makes right, and in a sense this brutal fact of life justified deceit and other means of avoidance to escape the dictates of authority and power. Fistfighting among boys was also approved, even encouraged, and we see later on in the descriptions of play the large role that fistfights occupied in connection with children's games. Fistfights were also an adult male form of recreation; whole villages or factory teams would square off against one another on the ice of a river and slug it out on Sundays or holidays.

The discussion of the different toys and games preferred by girls and boys leads naturally to consideration of sex role socialization. Semyonova sees this as achieved both by the conscious imposition of attitudes by grownups and by the children's observations of their parents' roles and power relationship.

*Semyonova speaks of the political structure of the peasant world. The land captaincy, established in 1889, was an important new element of this structure. Each rural precinct (*uchastok*) was assigned a land captain (*zemskii nachal'nik*), usually appointed from the nobility, to supervise peasant affairs. The land captain had extensive authority of both a judicial and an administrative character, including the right to review all decisions of the village commune (*mir*) as expressed through the decisions of the village assembly (*sel'skii skhod*).*[1] *The village assembly was formally an egalitarian gathering of all household heads (but in reality, as we will learn in a later chapter, subject to manipulation by the township supervisor* [volostnoi starshina] *and his allies). Each township (*volost'*) was supposed to have a rural police officer (*uriadnik*).*

Questions of political control and punishment suggest issues of religion and ultimate judgment. Semyonova, here and elsewhere, treats peasant views of religion with irony and condescension, pointing out their confusion about the role of God in the world and their mingling of pagan and Christian notions of holy days.

1. The powers of the land captains were considerably curtailed in 1906, following the revolution of 1905 and the granting to the peasants of civil rights equal to those of other classes.

Ivan's First Year

THE FOOD GIVEN to Ivan in his first year consists of breast milk, the *soska* or rag pacifier, kasha, bread, potatoes, and cow's milk. His mother is about the only person who concerns herself with his upbringing.

As soon as children develop teeth, they begin eating sour unripened apples and cucumbers.

Ivan's clothes consist of baby shirts. When his mother goes visiting or to mass, she wraps him in a blanket and covers his head with a little cap that she has sewn from scraps of cloth. A little girl would have a bonnet made from the same material.

The illnesses that Ivan is subject to in his first year include diarrhea, umbilical hernia, and scrofula (scabs on the head). Sometimes he suffers earaches, and in the summer he has infectious inflammation of the eyes, which is epidemic. Very small children suffer fevers, not to mention the usual children's diseases: whooping cough, tonsillitis, or diphtheria, measles, scarlet fever, and rashes. As a result of severe diarrhea, the intestines of small children sometimes extrude. Occasionally even little children have syphilis, inherited from their parents, although they may also acquire the disease through infection.[2] Midwives treat diarrhea in children by taking an affected child by the feet and shaking it head down. Women report that "the child screams and screams, but sometimes this method helps." For an umbilical hernia, the midwife will nibble at the navel of the child over the course of several days, or she might "let a mouse do the work" after she rubs the navel with dough. I know a case of a child dying from such treatment. Alternatively, she will apply wormwood to the navel.

2. Or so doctors at the time believed. Whether syphilis can be passed on in the promiscuous mingling of food and everyday living of the peasant household is a disputed question, but for an interesting discussion of its coded meanings for the moral outlook of Russian doctors, see Laura Engelstein, "Morality and the Wooden Spoon: Russian Doctors View Syphilis, Social Class, and Sexual Behavior, 1890-1905," *Representations*, 14 (Spring 1986), 169-208.

Still another way of treating hernia is to stand the child on its legs next to the door jamb and make a mark at the point where the jamb is level with the baby's navel. Then a hole is bored at that point with a gimlet. Scrofula is treated with bur marigold (*Bidens tripartia*). It is given to children to drink, and a brew of it is also added to a child's bath. To stop the recurrent crying of a colicky child, it is carried around the chicken coop.

Often children "dry out" from rickets, which is known as the "English disease." Another condition, a premature aging in children thought to be a form of rickets, is known to the peasants as "a dog's old age." Village healers use two treatments for it: baking the child in dough and giving the child a steam bath together with a dog.

By way of payment for these treatments, the midwife will take nearly anything of value, including bread, flour, groats, money, or soap. Bread dough is about the only thing she will not accept.

The peasants use the term *mladencheskaia* to refer to symptoms displayed by a child such as convulsions, spasms, and inflammation of the brain. They are convinced that everyone in childhood suffers from this *mladencheskaia.* Some children are thought to experience it when they are asleep, and so it is difficult to detect. This type is the most fortunate variety. The peasants believe that it is very dangerous to frighten a child when it is in the grip of *mladencheskaia,* for the child could easily become blind, deaf, or retarded. One peasant woman told me confidently that "it is well known that children die from two causes: diarrhea and *mladencheskaia.*"

Up to the time Ivan takes his first steps, he is looked after by his sister, a girl of nine or ten years of age.[3] She has difficulty carrying him around and often drops him, exclaiming: "Oops, my goodness! How did I let go of him?" Sometimes Ivan tumbles headfirst down a hillock. When he cries, his baby-sitter uses her free hand to slap him on the face or head, saying, "Keep quiet, you son of a bitch." Sometimes his sister leaves him on the ground, "at the

3. We are back to a composite picture of the peasant child Ivan now, for the excerpt on Ivan's real family does not speak of an older surviving sister.

Woman in bast shoes holds hand of one child, while a girl takes care of what may be her younger sibling. Village of Gorodnoe, Spassk district of Riazan province. Courtesy of the Riazan Museum.

softest spot around," and runs off to play with her friends or to catch crawfish in the river. For an hour or more, the child crawls around in the mud, wet, covered with dirt, and crying. To keep him quiet, he might be given a baked potato, an apple, or a cucumber. Sometimes he tries to climb over the high threshold of the house, falls, hurts himself, and bruises his face. Naturally, the baked potato or the cucumber he was given gets dragged through the dirt and thoroughly covered with mud and manure before he starts to eat it, sometimes well mixed with what is running out of his nose. He eats garbage from the pig trough, drinks from this same trough, and grabs hold of anything within reach, including his own feces. Sometimes he stuffs dirt in his mouth and swallows it.

The first things Ivan is aware of are, of course, hunger and satiety; later comes affection, indulgence, or whipping. His first words are "daddy," "mama," "nanny," "baba" (grandma). His first strivings are to grab anything that can be eaten. He recognizes his mother more than anyone else, and knows least of all his father, who pays less attention to him than do the other members of the family, except the uncles. I have observed generally that older fathers, though sometimes annoyed by the presence of children, are more affectionate with them than younger fathers. An elderly father or a grandfather is more likely to build a toy for a child or to take a child for a ride in the wagon than is a younger father. Parents, on returning from the market or a fair, usually bring the young children treats such as sunflower seeds or some cheap honey cakes or sugar candies. The children, impatient for their parents to return from the market, may occasionally go in a big group far down the road to meet them.

Ivan's Childhood to Age Six

When Ivan finally stood up "on his hind legs" and started to walk at about fourteen months, child care continued to be provided by his sister and mother. As before, he was often left in the charge of his sister, and the quality of her care changed only to the extent that she kicked him a bit harder for various offenses, such as screaming and dirtying his clothes. When he got hopelessly dirty, his sister would take off his shirt and send him to a large puddle or pond to wash up. Ivan would go off with the other children as naked as a jaybird and splash around in the water by the shore, the sun burning his back. When he ran naked back to his sister, as a reward for his obedience she dressed him again in his shirt, which had had time to dry out on a pole. When mother was at home, she washed him herself. She would also scrub his shirt, patch it on occasion, pick the lice off his head, and give him better pieces of food than he would receive from his sister. As a result, he naturally clung most closely to his mother.

As far as Ivan's getting fed on time, the only one who cares about this is [again] his mother, and she cares but little.[4] She calls the children to dinner and supper when the grownups sit down to eat, but if the children do not appear, she does not worry much about it. "It's all the same," she says, "even if they eat some now, they'll run off again to play and then come back to ask for food a second time. They eat us out of house and home!" Some mothers report that their children eat on the run; that is, whenever it strikes their fancy, they go to their mothers and ask for a piece of bread to munch on. Consequently, the principal food of peasant children is dry bread and potatoes. When their mother is away from the house, the children go hungry.

It happens that children of about four to six years of age, when unsupervised, will sometimes eat henbane or nightshade (*Solanum nigrum*), referred to by peasants as *bznika* [a narcotic and, in large enough doses, deadly plant]. The children may also approach a horse from behind and grab it by the tail or whip it with a twig. This frequently costs them a disfigured face, broken teeth, and injured eyes. The same little children are the cause of fires: in the absence of their parents, they grab a pack of matches and light a bonfire in the yard, or next to the threshing barn, and in no time the whole village burns down.

4. This paragraph is from Semyonova's field notes in Arkhiv AN SSSR, f. 906, op. 1, d. 26, l. 305.

Children begin to climb from the age of two. At first, they climb on a bench. Later they clamber over the gates and wattle fencing. They fall down headfirst and hurt themselves. The smallest children sometimes crawl from the bench [attached to the inside wall of the house] up to the window and fall out the window. Children who are a little older will climb the threshing barn and the trees, and they do not always escape injury. For this mischief the children are punished by the grownups.

Fistfighting and swearing are learned quite early. As soon as Ivan began to walk, he started fighting with other children. He was actually encouraged to do this, especially if he was able to best another small child. Ivan learned swear words from his older brothers and sisters, even before he could put together a complete sentence. He started to call his mother a bitch whenever she denied him something, much to the delight of the whole family, even the mother herself. They would actually encourage him on such occasions. "You sly little rascal." "So this is what your mother is when she does not listen to you." Mothers sometimes naively boast of the talent of their young children, saying, "What an ataman he is, already calling me a bitch!" To be an ataman [literally: a Cossack chieftain] means to lead other children in brawling or starting mischief. Ivan sometimes hit his mother on the apron with a twig, to the amusement of the grownups. As far as swear words go, all the children, beginning with the very youngest, know almost the entire repertoire of abusive peasant words. Needless to say, boys of seven to twelve years of age, and even girls of the same age, swear and use foul language during their play (when they are quarreling). "Cur, bitch, bastard, whore" are swear words frequently used by children.

At the age Ivan started to walk, his clothing consisted of homespun or linen shirts, worn as a gown or belted at the waist. His hair was blond and, naturally, uncombed, and cut in a circle. His feet were bare, with a caked-on crust of black earth. For Communion his mother dressed him in a cleaner shirt made from domestic linen dyed blue and carefully belted it. On such an occasion, he would wear stockings made of wool and woolen cloth shoes. She also made sure to rub his head with butter or vegetable oil. When a boy turns two, he is fitted out with trousers, likewise made from homespun fabric. But boys begin to wear trousers all the time only at age eight or ten. Little girls are also clad only in linen shirts, but longer shirts than those of the boys, and always belted at the waist. Very early, from about age two, they like to tie a kerchief around their heads. On holidays the girls are dressed in calico sarafans. Girls from the age of about ten usually wear homespun skirts even at home. On occasion, the girls also put on woolen stockings and shoes.

Punishment for mischief consisted of beatings administered by the parents. They beat Ivan for screaming, getting covered with mud, or stealing a piece of food. They did not beat him for fighting, lying, or using foul language. His father most often beat him for screaming, while his mother beat him mainly for screaming or ruining his clothes. They hit him with their hands, with whips, or with switches, and pulled his ears and hair.

The mischief of two- or three-year-old boys amounts mostly to damaging their clothes or stealing pieces of food that they can immediately stuff in their mouths. Ivan would receive a cuff on the back of his head if he got in the way. He was, however, a very good dodger and knew how to jump back in time and scamper out of range of a slap that was intended for him. They beat him if he climbed up to where he might fall and hurt himself. One four-year-old urchin, having gotten the idea that he could take the place of a hen, sat on a hen's nest with little chicks. When his mother found him there, she had to act so as not to frighten him, for he might smother all the chicks. "What a nice hen I have here!" she declared. Hearing this, the child let her come closer and take him from the nest, after which he was, of course, beaten with a rope and received a few pulls on his hair. In another case, a few children climbed to the very top of a barn. Their father, not wishing to frighten them into falling off, coaxed them into coming down "to drink tea" (a rare treat). When the children were safely down, they were treated not to tea but to a thrashing with leather straps.

Ivan learned to lie as soon as he understood the connection between his actions and punishment. For lying he was not punished at all. So he lied out of self-defense and to gain the time needed to escape his parents' anger. He might place the blame on a neighbor and so be able to run away, while his mother went looking for the alleged culprit. He knew perfectly well that his parents' anger would subside if he managed to stay out sight for a few hours. To convince the parents of their innocence, even the youngest children will swear impressive oaths. It is safe to say that children master the art of lying out of fear being beaten.

Ivan during Preadolescence and Teenage

Little children grow up very quickly in peasant life. It is not uncommon for a ten-year-old to reason like an adult. This is mainly because of the uncomplicated nature of peasant affairs, and also the child's participation in most of the work and in all of the activities of peasant life, in which everything is out in the open. Adults are not constrained by the presence of children from speaking about anything they like, getting drunk, or fighting. Having experienced hunger since his early years, a child soon learns to appreciate the value of things. Little Ivan understands perfectly what it means when his father spends money in a tavern and how it will affect the child's own well-being. Frequently Ivan will reproach his mother or father in such instances. If he fails to do so consistently, it is only from fear of being beaten.

Seeing that brute force constantly triumphs, Ivan begins very early to recognize that might makes right. If his father beats his mother, then he naturally feels sorry for her, but not in the sense that his father is wrong and his mother is right. He feels sorry for his mother either instinctively or because "daddy may end up killing her." And to lose a mother is the most terrible misfortune for a child. It is the mother more than the father who rears the children. A mother will give her all to get her children on their feet and bring up her son to be a helper for her. A father, on the other hand, behaves with remarkable unconcern for his orphaned children. No children are more unfortunate than those without a mother. For the father, it is as if the children did not exist, and stepmothers beat and abuse them.

A peasant child's attitude toward the rural authorities, toward doctors and folk healers, is the same as that of grownups. Children do not have their own special way of thinking about these people. If little Ivan is asked, "Why was the land captaincy established?" he answers, "To keep us peasants down." In some remote villages, far from the *zemstvo* station, a child will know personally only the rural police officer, and being well aware of his father's needs [that is, the peasant's need to be suspicious of any outsider], the child will perceive the land captain, the district supervisor, and the governor as a single entity.

A child's conception of the world differs little in essence from that of adults, with the exception that, for a child, parental authority plays a big role. Little Ivan cannot, of course, conceive how he could live without the power of his parents, who at any time can punish or beat him but who also feed him. (Even mothers will beat their sons.) Little Ivans are keenly aware of their dependence on their parents. Our children are no less dependent on their parents than are peasant children, but because they are well fed, they feel it less.

As concerns the authorities, the communal organization, and nature, every ten-year-old knows as much about them as his elders, since he is around them constantly and attends their gatherings. As for nature, little Ivans have more leisure time than adults to observe it. From this, it seems easy enough to draw some conclusions about a child's conception of the world. The world naturally seems scarier and more grandiose to children than to adults. From natural phenomena such as thunder and severe storms to mysterious ones such as God and the prophets, or disasters such as house fires, all appear more terrifying to the peasant child than to an adult. And just as with our children, little Ivans feel relief from their fears when their parents are near. Maybe peasant children experience greater fears, owing to tales about changelings, witches, house-spirits, and wood-goblins, which the adults, too, believe. Nevertheless, when little Ivans are under the wing of their mothers or other protective adults, they feel more or less out of danger. "Hush, hush! Don't cry—I won't give you away," is the constant reassurance offered by a mother or father when a child is terrified and crying. Peasant youngsters with drunken and abusive parents are very frightened children of a kind we do not have. For that reason, peasant children [in this situation] are always mistrustful when someone beckons to them (even their own parents), suspecting a mean trick instead of a caress. I mentioned earlier how parents, fearing that a child might run off, lure him so as to teach him a lesson for some misdeed.

Punishment of children in the seven-to-eleven-year-old age group occurs, as has been mentioned earlier, for theft and other offenses that either threaten the well-being of the child or cause damage to the household (accidental arson, spilled milk, broken dishes, and so on). They are punished mainly with beatings by means of a rope, cattle switch, nettles, fists, feet, or pulling on the ears and hair. Sometimes as a punishment a child is denied lunch or dinner. Very little children (age four) are tied with rope to a table leg or a bench for several hours.

[It is also interesting to observe] when children first learn about God and the saints, and what conception children have of their significance, whether they are good or evil, or frightening, whether they are always interfering in people's lives and affairs, and how they concern the child. Up to the age of two, or sometimes three, children have no idea about God, but gradually they begin to understand that the icons in the corner of the house are "God." Imitating their elders, they cross themselves in front of the icons.

By the age of seven a child may learn how to repeat some of the "Our Father" and the "Hail Mary" prayers. There are, however, women who never manage to master the words of the "Our Father." The first words a child hears about God are, naturally, that "God will punish you." Therefore, the child imagines God first and foremost as a threatening presence. The first saint that children hear about is Elijah the Prophet. They very early begin to cross themselves when they hear thunder so that Elijah [the Thunderbolt] will not kill them. At confession, to which children go from the age of six or seven, the priest also frightens them with the idea of punishment from God. However, as little Ivan grows up and starts to participate in herding and in pranks in common with other children, or when he enters school, he soon becomes infected with "free-thinking." Children frequently say, "You never know if God will punish you or not." Such "free-thinking," in both children and adults, is surprisingly enough combined with religious faith and superstition. Children hear from their elders about Yegor the protector of the horses; Agrafena-kupal'nitsa [a mythical figure associated with the first summer river bathing in the north on the eve of Ivan Day (June 23)]; Aleksei "s gor potoki" [associated with the spring thaw festival celebrated on March 17]; and John the Baptist. All these stories are fairly well known.

The name day of Saints Cyril and Methodius in May is referred to here as "Tsar-Grad—Cyril and Methodius" [as if Tsar-Grad, which means "imperial city" and is often associated with Constantinople, were the name of a person]. People are not supposed to work on this day, because "Tsar-Grad is a stern father who may destroy the crops."[5] A child, of course, listens to all these tales and repeats them word for word.

The first responsibilities and chores given to Ivan consist of taking care of his younger brothers and sisters. Like a sister, a brother is sometimes required to rock the cradle. Older sisters like to turn their responsibilities over to their younger brothers and run off to their friends. I am familiar with the case of an older sister, a girl about twelve years old, who ran off to her friends and left her sick ten-month-old sister, suffering with diarrhea, in the care of two boys, ages five and six. The boys rocked the cradle so hard that

5. The phrase contains a pun so obvious in Russian that Semyonova does not need to explain it. *Grad* in Russian (besides being an archaic form of the word for city) means "hail," as in the destructive weather phenomenon. "Emperor Hail" would naturally pose a threat to crops.

the baby flew out, struck her head on a stone in the earthen floor, and died instantly.

[The actual story of this tragedy, which I found in the archive among Semyonova's field notes and which also includes observations of theft, is as follows:][6] My painting gives me frequent opportunity to observe various village scenes. The other day I was painting in the gardens of one of the far corners of the village of M. Two peasant women stood by the barn.

"This morning I went out to the garden, dearie, and discovered that someone had dug up my potatoes. They had stolen half of one bed. . . . Fie on them!"

"All right, then, my dear, I'm going to let you know who did it," the other woman says, lowering her voice. "I can't say absolutely for sure, but the day before yesterday I heard with my own ears how Afinia Grynikhina was hitting their Dunka and yelling at her, saying, 'You can't even dig up a few potatoes for dinner, for Pete's sake, you bungler!' You know what kind of potatoes they have, and so, it's clear that Dunka went over to your garden. But just don't tell anyone that I told you about this. . . ."

At that moment, Dunka appeared on the street carrying a pail. The woman who had lost her potatoes ran over and started swearing at her. Dunka, a thin girl with a snub nose and tearful black eyes, is never at a loss for words. The noise of their voices alerted Dunka's aunt, Afinia, who ran out of her house, and a real scrap got going, to the point that it made your ears ring. In the midst of this, a seven-year-old boy all in tears approached the group of loudly cursing women [and said,] "Dunka, come to the house quick; Katka is hurt!" The fight quieted down for a second. From the house came the scream of a child. Dunka took off on a run for the house, from which after an instant she bolted with a howl. "Katka's dead. Oh, people, how can this have happened!" Everyone streamed toward the place it had occurred. Katka (Dunka's young sister), an emaciated one-year-old girl who had just recovered from dysentery, had indeed been killed, having fallen from a

6. Arkhiv AN SSSR, f. 906, op. 1, d. 26, l. 308.

crib hung from a fairly high spot. She evidently fell headfirst and smashed her temple on a rock lying on the home's earthen floor and then and there surrendered her soul to God. Her little cousins had gone into the house and seen the child on the floor with a smashed temple. They checked and found that she was dead. Then one of them let out a childish howl; the other went out to summon the warring women.[7]

Little Ivan is not averse to abusing his younger brothers, whereas he fears his older brothers. He nevertheless feels some sympathy for his youngest siblings, the toddlers, and often shares his apples, cookies, and cucumbers with them.

Also, little Ivan is sometimes expected to perform tasks beyond his abilities, such as fetching a heavy pail of water from the well. He tends his father's horse. In our village, the peasants do not keep a paid shepherd for all the horses of the community. Each peasant householder sends his young son (age seven to eleven) to graze the family's horse in a fallow field or ravine, or on the field margins. Naturally, during this type of grazing, all the little boys of the village band together "in a drove" and get into mischief. Their favorite pranks are to find a bird's nest and bake the eggs from it in a campfire, and to pick mushrooms, nuts, and berries in woods belonging to someone else. Sometimes the whole group will decide to leave two boys to look after the horses while the rest sneak into the landowner's garden and steal apples or go into the backyards of the villagers and cut off the heads of all the sunflowers and stuff cucumbers in their shirts. On one occasion, the boys stole a goose from the miller, cut it up, roasted it in the fire, and ate it. They often steal ducks and roast them.

Girls also tend the farm animals; they usually are in charge of the calves. Our calves are grazed separately from the cows. Every household in turn must tend to the village calves for one day. Sometimes the women do this work, but in the majority of cases

7. The field note, which ends here, evidently gives the boys' version of what happened and does not square with the story in the published study of the boys' rough rocking of the cradle. Did Semyonova learn the true story later, or did she perhaps embellish the story in her finished draft?

they send a girl, nine to twelve years old, to tend the herd. Since the calves usually graze near the village in a dell or pasture, several of the young shepherdess's friends will accompany her. The girls naturally behave better than the boys; they might organize a game of jacks or sew something, and sometimes they sing songs. The young, pre-teenage shepherds usually stay away from the girls, except to tease or to frighten them. But if the boys grazing the horses include youngsters fourteen to sixteen years of age, they carry on more outrageously than the younger boys. Their antics make an older girl "ashamed even to walk past them," for they greet her with quite unrestrained words and jokes.

They smoke "cigarettes" made from scraps of paper. Some of them begin smoking at the age of eight. Boys sixteen and seventeen years old buy tobacco for the cigarettes in a general store or a tavern and pay for it with eggs stolen from their mothers. About twenty-five years ago, the youngsters smoked pipes, but now they smoke "cigarettes." They smoke the strong, homegrown tobacco known as *makhorka,* which they buy at the shop in the village for three kopecks per 1.8 ounces. They also buy paper there of various types, which is second-hand, in many cases newsprint. Sometimes paper is obtained, as they say, "around the homes of the landlords." The average peasant spends three to three and a half rubles a year on smoking.

Boys and girls seven to ten years old are sent to drive the cattle in and to clip grass for the cows. They are also sent to the tavern for liquor. Boys age seven to eleven cart sheaves and harvest potatoes. Girls first work as baby-sitters, then in the field, weeding, digging potatoes, and carrying drinks to the adults during the field-work season. They rinse the linens. They learn to sew and spin, and to scutch the flax and hemp. They fetch water.

Incidentally, in the summer, children love going in large groups for a swim in the river. They pick out a shallow place and stay in the water all day. They begin swimming as early as April and continue right up to September. Girls are just as fond of swimming as are the boys, and they often swim along with the boys, who love to tease them and run off with their shifts and

Five boys of various ages from Bobrov district of Voronezh province, south of Riazan. Photo by A. I. Prishvits from *Rossiia. Polnoe geograficheskoe opisanie,* vol. 2, p. 186.

Russian children frolicking in the water of the Volga River. Courtesy of the Library of Congress.

sarafans and hide them in the bushes. Frequently the children play so long in the water that their mothers have to chase them out with nettles or a cattle switch.

In their treatment of dogs, cats, and other animals, Ivan and his family can be rather cruel. They will spare a horse or a cow mainly because it is work power and in this sense an important asset. This still does not prevent a drunken peasant from venting his anger on his horse when he gets mad. He will thrash its side and muzzle if the animal does not have the strength to pull the cart. As for cats and dogs, these animals are not much valued, and so with them peasants are not too particular. Cats and dogs are also less useful than other animals, and peasants will torture them just for the fun of it, just to see what will happen. Little children like to throw cats and puppies, when they can catch them, into the water to see if they can swim. When I ask, "Don't you feel sorry for them?" the children respond: "Why feel sorry? They're not people, just dogs."

Here is a short, rather typical account that reveals two aspects of the child Ivan. A boy of about eight years of age found a puppy hereabouts, and when his mother, a widow, would not let him keep it, he hid it in a hole in the threshing barn and regularly took it something to eat (he shared his own food with the puppy). In time the puppy, which turned out to be female, came out of hiding. At first the boy's mother shut her eyes to this, but when male dogs started to visit the female, the mother began to lose patience, and once, when some of the other boys were present, she said to her son, "Go hang your bitch, you fool, before these dogs eat us alive!" The boys picked up on this and discussed the ferocity of dogs during the mating season. Little by little the other boys began to tease Fedka, saying that he could not hang his bitch when she was surrounded by the other dogs, which would, of course, tear apart anyone who got near her. Finally, they drove Fedka to desperation in defense of his honor. "What do you mean I won't hang her?" he cried. "I'm not at all afraid of those dogs!" "Okay," said the other boys, "hang her, then, and we will believe you." Fedka picked up a rope, caught the bitch, and led her to the willows by the river bank, followed by a train of children and dogs. Along the way the boys naturally continued to egg him on. At the river, the boy hung the feeble little dog from a branch. But the rope was rotten and broke, and the dog, which was still alive, fell down and floundered in the river. The children began to laugh. Altogether beside himself because of the laughter and his own failure, Fedka grabbed a handful of stones and used them to finish off the half-dead dog, with which earlier he had shared his bread. After killing the dog, he began to feel bad about it and headed home. "Where are you going, Fedka?" the children asked. "There is nothing to see here!" he replied angrily. The rest of the boys looked on unconcernedly, or, more accurately, with morbid curiosity, as one of the male dogs plunged into the river, pulled out the dead dog, and dragged it through the backyards.

During the plowing, peasants love to swear at their horses. This does no harm to the horses, of course, and so it is comical to hear a stream of foul language pouring out at some poor gelding or mare. "Oh, oh, you louse . . . move! You devil, you rotter, dog's shit!" On these occasions, the peasants swear with gusto, with pure joy, with delight, and probably sometimes just for the fun of listening to themselves. To swear at animals is no sin, or hardly a sin.

[Games form an important part of children's lives.] Up to the age of ten, boys and girls sometimes play together. Their favorite games are catch, "wattle fence," and "radish."

In "wattle fence," children stand in a row and intertwine their arms like a wattle fence. The boy or girl who is "it," or in this case the "firebug," approaches the child at the end of the "fence." "Vanka, give me a light!" Sometimes Vanka refuses. Then the firebug goes to the other end. "Aniska, give me a light!" She holds out a wooden stick, the "match." The "firebug" then walks along the "fence" pretending to strike the match and light the "fence," after which he runs off. The "wattle fence" unravels, and the children all try to catch the firebug. When they do, they beat him.

"Radish" begins with the children squatting in a long row, each holding the belt of the one in front of him or her. Someone proceeds to "pull out a radish." This person goes up to the first child in the row and says, "Give me some radishes, old woman." The speaker then takes the squatting child by the hand and tries to pull him to his feet while the next child holds on from behind, preventing him from rising. The person playing the radish says, "It is hard for you to pull me out, and so you should dig me out." The child takes a stick and digs around the radish. But again the radish cannot be pulled out. The "radish" says, "Water me." The child brings water in some kind of crock pot and pours it on the radish (to the amusement of all). "Shake me," the "radish" says, and so it goes. Finally, the radish is pulled out, and the child tries the next one. If all the radishes are overpowered, then the boy or girl who did it is "the champ" (although the champ's arms hurt all day from this exercise).

Boys a little older (ten to twelve) play ball. They stand in a circle holding sticks, and on the ground in front of each player is a hole. One boy stands in the middle of the circle holding a stick and a ball crudely fashioned out of wood. He tries to hit or putt the ball into the hole of one of the boys while the boy being challenged tries to beat the ball away. If the one who is "it" succeeds in getting the ball into one of the holes, he trades places with the boy defending that hole. The bare legs of the boys sometimes become very sore from being hit by the ball and the sticks, and the boys can end up coming to blows, occasionally fighting fiercely and even drawing blood. Girls do not play ball and, of course, do not get into fistfights. They like to play with rag dolls, and they sometimes have the dolls stand for "masters" who beat their workers, or they will marry two of the dolls, and the like.

Peasant children have an excellent ability to imitate, especially other people's speech and expressions, and in their play they sometimes pretend to be "the little masters" and imitate the children of the landlords. I recall from my childhood how we observed from my garden the peasant children playing "little masters": that is, they were pretending to be us. They were very good at simulating our voices and even our manner of speaking.[8]

In the winter, the children's favorite activities are sledding and skating. They spend entire days running on frozen puddles, ponds, and streams, skating on their feet. If the weather is so cold or their clothes so poor that they have to stay indoors, the girls play dolls and the boys play knucklebones. Given the close confines of the house, this game can lead to the boys' bumping into and pushing one another, and in the heat of a match they sometimes break out into fisticuffs.[9]

8. The above paragraph is from Semyonova's field notes in Arkhiv AN SSSR, f. 906, op. 1, d. 26, l. 304.
9. The above paragraph is from an unpublished typescript of Semyonova's work in AGO, f. 109, op. 1, d. 170, ch. 5, l. 4.

Children sitting in the yard playing a game of *kamushki,* in which little stones are cast. Village of Lokash, Spassk district of Riazan province. Courtesy of the Riazan Museum.

Boys playing a game of *kazanki* in the street. Village of Seit-ovo, Kasimov district of Riazan province. Courtesy of the Riazan Museum.

Children's toys are very simple. Fathers make the children small wooden carts, with which the older children give the younger ones rides, and in which the girls cart around their rag dolls. Boys have whips to play with. At fairs the children buy clay whistles in the shape of birds. Boys sometimes ride hobby horses. For the girls the best fun is new clothes. A three-year-old girl who has been given shoes or a shawl cannot be separated from them even at night. A girl will always value a new sarafan over an elegantly dressed doll.

Relations between boys and girls and their understanding of the difference between the sexes [are early inculcated by the attitudes of the grownups]. Adults often jokingly refer to very young children as "brides and grooms." Even the youngest children attend betrothals and weddings. On the other hand, they very early come to understand the material side of their daily life. The father is master of the house and the mother the mistress. The father has command over the mother, and the mother has specific duties and responsibilities. So every child well understands that girls are future "brides" and boys future "grooms." In some villages, even today the custom exists to promise very young girls (aged twelve to fourteen) to boys of corresponding age (for example, in Ol'khi and Zabolot'e, two villages of the Dankov district of Riazan province). The parents of the children have a drink on the deal, and they begin to refer to one another as "matchmakers" [a term that also connotes in-law status in Russian] and to pay visits to each other. Nowadays betrothals of this type are often nullified when the boys and girls get older. But if not, such fourteen- or fifteen-year-old brides and sixteen-year-old grooms begin to live together before they reach majority. This happens, of course, only after a big party.

Ivan is sent off to school when he is ten. "He'll be better paid if he can read and write," say the peasants. Nowadays, in view of the wages paid in Moscow, more and more peasants are endeavoring to have their sons learn reading and writing. They say such things as: "In Moscow it is more important than here to know reading and writing, and you are judged by your knowledge of it," and "It is harder to cheat a literate person."

A boy soon finds an opportunity to put his literacy to use. He writes letters for the old folks and often gets awarded one or two kopecks for his service. He may also read the Psalter prayers for the dead for forty kopecks a night. Although the boys do not forget how to read and write after they leave school, their writing may become more illegible and contain more misspellings as time goes on; they naturally tend to lose command of the rules of grammar and arithmetic. The historical or geographical knowledge conveyed in school is quickly forgotten, since it has no application in daily life. I remarked nevertheless that when prompted, the children recall some of this information. They especially like poems and memorize them easily, and seem to be fascinated with rhymes, without giving much thought to their content. This past fall, a book about the end of the world (a collision between Earth and a comet) was widely circulated and much discussed.

For some reason, school fails to change the peasants' view of the life around them. There is school and then there is life, and in the minds of the peasants a line always divides the two. Our village has a reading room. Boys and young men like to take out books. The biggest demand is for novels (Gogol is very popular) or for anything "amusing." The demand for historical novels and the lives of saints is not as great, while books about nature and husbandry are never requested.

Our area has only one state school and some parochial schools. The program of the state school is very comprehensive (two grades, five sections, five years of study), and rarely does anyone finish the school. The program of the parish schools (one grade for two years, two grades for four years, and a two-year grammar school) is as follows: Catechism, Church Slavic, choir, Russian, counting, introduction to geography and Russian history. Here are some excerpts from the program (1894 edition):

> The very name parochial schools points to the special importance of Catechism in their curriculum. It is the principal subject, and an effort

> should be made to relate all other subjects to it as closely as possible. In accordance with the goals and the spirit of instruction, Church Slavic language should be taught in conjunction with the Catechism, as its closest auxiliary discipline, and should have precedence immediately after it. In the teaching of Russian, the emphasis should be on study of the language itself and not on other things, such as conveying information about the secular world. Introduction to Russian history, being inseparable from the history of the Russian church, should be taught together with the latter. From the general course of Russian history, the pupils should derive the firm conviction that our motherland has always drawn its strength from the Orthodox faith and autocratic tsarist rule, and that whenever the people's faith weakened or autocratic rule faltered, the Russian land was exposed to terrible misfortunes and came close to destruction.

Instructors at the parochial schools are priests, deacons, and sometimes lay teachers, the last being peasants who graduated from parish schools. The instructors commonly resort to corporal punishment of their pupils. The schoolboys do not like to study Church Slavic grammar. In schools in which one priest has to handle all the teaching on his own, the business usually goes badly. A school like this in Kobel'sha is worthless, in the opinion of the peasants. "The priest teaches one day, and takes off two."[10]

Ivan's chores after school consist of plowing, learning to mow, transporting sheaves, and looking after the horses; in a word, he already helps his father with everything. He might have to do day labor or work for a neighboring landowner to pay off a debt incurred by his father.

If a young Ivan is not in school, he is often a shepherd on hire. When a shepherd is hired by the village council, the council

10. It is clear from Semyonova's notes about her project that she intended to describe peasant schooling and its impact in great detail, but she was evidently unable to do this before she died. See *Zapiski RGO*, 122. A recent, very thorough study of Russian peasant schools in this era is Ben Eklof, *Russian Peasant Schools: Officialdom, Village Culture, and Popular Pedagogy, 1861-1914* (Berkeley: University of California Press, 1986).

This appears to be a village school, judging from the urban dress of the woman on the stairway, probably a teacher. Photo is identified only as a group of peasants from the village of Fedot´evo, Spassk district of Riazan province. Courtesy of the Riazan Museum.

usually receives a gift from the candidate of a quarter- or half-pail of vodka [from five to ten bottles]. It sometimes happens that the council members drink up the vodka on one candidate's account and then find some fault for which they can dismiss him, but they actually do it to get free drinks from another fellow.

The peasants hire a boy of ten or twelve years old as their shepherd or, better, herdsboy. Hiring a herdsboy for the common herd involves the following conditions: the shepherd pays the boy from his own salary seven to nine rubles for the whole summer (six months), and during this period all the households take turns feeding the boy. A household that has "one share" provides board for one day, those with "two shares" provide board for two days, and so on. A cow is considered "one share"; ten sheep likewise constitute "one share." A heifer in the first field counts the same as two sheep, while a heifer in the second field equals four sheep. The shepherd himself receives thirty-five rubles for the whole summer if the herd is not very large and needs only one herdsboy, and fifty to sixty rubles if the herd is large and requires the services of two herdsboys. Before the cattle are put out to pasture, the shepherd collects eggs from the peasants, two eggs and a handful of soaked hemp per share. Twice a year, on Coronation Day and Christmas, the shepherd collects one pie (pirog) from each household. He gets his board in the same way as the herdsboy, by going from house to house.

Landowners hire herdsboys for the summer at eight to twelve rubles plus board. A boy who herds cows receives eight rubles, while one who looks after horses earns ten to twelve rubles.

[Now let us look at Ivan's earnings and terms of work if he hires on not as a herdsboy but as a farm worker.] Both peasants and landlords pay a farm worker from twenty-seven to thirty-five rubles plus board for a summer, i.e., from March until the Advent fast beginning on November 15. A year-long worker is paid between forty and fifty-five rubles and free board likewise. Women farm workers are paid from twenty-four to thirty-six rubles a year. Each farm worker makes a contract with the landlord, which is signed in the presence of witnesses in the district office. The contract is kept by the employer, while the worker has a booklet in which the payments and fines he or she has received are entered.[11] Workers are fined for drunkenness, for unauthorized absenteeism on a work day, or for damage to the farm's property (horses and equipment) resulting from carelessness on their part that can be confirmed by eyewitnesses. They are also fined for rude remarks to the boss.[12] Merchants more often than others fine workers for

11. See the appendix for an example of such a work contract.
12. See below an example of litigation over this issue (p. 162).

rudeness. Daily pay varies widely. In years with good crops, men are paid twenty-five to fifty kopecks per day during the field-work season, and women are paid twenty to forty kopecks. In poor years, men are paid twenty to thirty-five kopecks per day, women fifteen to twenty-five kopecks. In the winter, for one working day men are paid fifteen to thirty kopecks, women ten to twenty-five.

[Some idea of the purchasing power of these wages can be obtained from the following list of prices for basic items of clothing:] woman's shift, 1.8 to 2.5 rubles; warm cloth shoes, 3 rubles; woman's shirt, 1 ruble; stockings, 30 kopecks; long-waisted jacket for women made of homespun, 5 rubles; man's shirt, 50 kopecks; man's jacket, 5 rubles; felt boots, 2.2 rubles; leather boots, 7.5 rubles.

4

COURTSHIP AND SEXUAL RELATIONS

Most ethnographic accounts of Russian villagers in the nineteenth century indicate fairly strong sanctions against premarital intercourse. Standards for extramarital intercourse were more flexible for married women or even for unmarried women of the age of most married women. Attitudes apparently varied from place to place as well, and, as Semyonova's descriptions reveal, they were changing rapidly in the late nineteenth century under the impact of migrant labor and rising age at first marriage.

Despite the power of men to force women to submit, some of the stories in this chapter demonstrate the degree of control that women could exercise over sexual relations and, as noted earlier in connection with the lying-over deaths of infants, the ultimate responsibility and control that women maintained in the area of family planning. I should, however, note that, although I have no evidence with which to challenge her story of the Easter Sunday infanticide, the account has a folkloric quality in its report of the murder of an innocent on the eve of Easter and its subsequent discovery (resurrection). Another Russian collector of ethnographic information at about the same time reported a popular story of a widow who became pregnant and killed her illegitimate child on Easter, though this story was embellished with many magical and surreal elements.[1]

1. A. V. Balov, "O paskhe," *Zhivaia Starina*, 4:2 (1896), 260-61.

At the close of the chapter, Semyonova discusses "wayward women" with words suggesting that, whereas in the past her villagers did not tolerate premarital relations among unengaged couples, a young woman with only one lover was no longer regarded as "wayward." Even here she seems to refer to a village that was already under the influence of urban values; the story that follows about a remote village indicates rather severe sanctions against premarital pregnancy, suggesting again that attitudes varied widely. Pregnancy is different from sexual relations, it is true, but the moral stance in both cases would be closely related.

❖

THE AGE AT WHICH girls start to consider Ivan "eligible," that is, someone who is admitted to parties and dances and who can be an object of their "love," usually depends on the boy's looks and height. Sometimes a tall, handsome sixteen-year-old boy is considered a full-fledged "groom"—a boy who can bestow his favors on the girls—whereas an underdeveloped eighteen-year-old may be rejected. In general, short people are the objects of ridicule. Small men and women are given nicknames such as "birdie," "runt," "shrimp," "puppy." "A little dog is forever a pup," the girls will mock a small, unattractive man.

In the past, there were quite a few inexperienced boys and girls, but nowadays "innocent" boys are not to be found, and even girls without experience are rather few. A boy of sixteen or seventeen years of age usually has a girlfriend. The two become acquainted, as a rule, at the spring or summer street gatherings and at evening parties. Beginning at Easter, girls gather outdoors for singing and dancing. From then until the start of winter, outdoor gatherings are held on all holidays and occasionally even on workdays. At the country (round) dances, boys choose girls and kiss them, dancing to the sound of a pipe and an accordion. They sometimes dance in pairs—the quadrille. When the older people have gone to bed, whoever chooses to do so goes off to the haystacks, the bushes, or the threshing barns, and there matters proceed to sexual relations. More or less the same thing happens at parties; young people might wander off to a barn or a shed.

Parents, of course, frequently upbraid and even whip their daughters for these liaisons. The boys, in contrast, are not punished. Boys naturally look upon premarital liaisons more lightly than girls, and boys frequently break off relations with the girls "they have loved." But quite often these premarital affairs lead to marriage. In villages in which parents still adhere to the custom of arranging marriages and do not give their children a choice, young people become involved with the purpose of confirming their intention to get married. In these instances, parents agree more readily to their son's choice if he tells them that he and his chosen one have already "sinned" and in this sense have pledged to be faithful unto death. If a boy has already proposed and the "bride-show" (*smotriny*)[2] has taken place, then even the older folks look indulgently on premarital relations between the betrothed. Lately this is almost becoming the custom.

When a boy becomes intimate with a girl, he naturally assures her that he is going to marry her. But once in a while you run across a boy who is under the influence of city values and will make his real intentions clear to the girl right from the start: "I'll love you only as long as I want to: no promises." Most girls, however, hope to marry the boys they are going with.

If the youth is a live-in farm laborer, getting a woman is even easier, and usually a married one at that. If he is a farm laborer in a peasant's household, he is likely to take up with one of the women of the house, a family member, and if he is working for a large landlord, his sweetheart may be a cook for the workers, a cattle-yard worker, or the like. Hired cooks usually have the reputation of being "loose women." I knew a woman about thirty years old who worked as a cook while her husband was away on seasonal

2. This custom of inspecting the bride and the households of the marital couple some days prior to the wedding is described in detail in chapter 6.

work; she was said to be dating eight workers at a time. This sort of thing could happen only while the people were employed at the estate of a landlord [and thus away from the scrutiny of their neighbors]. People between the ages of sixteen and forty hire on for such seasonal jobs with large landlords. Each of the woman's lovers knew well that there were seven others. Sometimes, when speaking calmly among themselves, they would decide that they should get together and teach her a lesson, but they never got around to carrying out this plan; she apparently knew how to soft-soap every one of them.

The street parties (*ulitsa*) are attended by girls from the whole village as well as by young women, especially those whose husbands are away. They dress up and at dusk go out to a pasture, thus distancing themselves from the supervision of the community (*poriadok*). They begin with some long drawn-out songs of the type sung in connection with country dances. These gatherings attract not only local girls but also young people from neighboring villages. If there is a landowner's estate nearby, the farm laborers are among the first to arrive at the street party, together with female cooks, shepherdesses, and others. They come with accordions and shepherd's pipes, which provide accompaniment for the dancing that takes place after they have gotten drunk. The more frantic the dancing becomes, the more daring are the verses women sing as accompaniment. "My husband is a devil, but I am not afraid of him." "Oh what misery, with my husband Grigorii! I'd even take a skinny one as long as his name is Ivan!" "I did not give my sweetheart enough love, caressing him and kissing him." Some women sing even more embarrassing ditties to the delight and cheers of the company. As it gets later, few people remain. One or two men, having "warmed up" at a bootleg liquor joint, dance to the music of the accordion. The rest disperse in pairs to the bushes and behind the barns. These parties sometimes continue until two in the morning, even though the field-work season may be on. The people nap for an hour or two and then go off to the field.

[During the cold and inclement weather after the work season, the parties move indoors.] These "evening parties" (*vechorki*, *vecherinki*) proceed as follows: the young women arrange with some widow or soldier's wife who lives alone to use her house for the night, with one or two pints of kerosene offered as payment to cover lighting expenses. The parties are frequented by unmarried women, soldiers' wives, and women whose husbands are away. Every party is presided over by an "elder" (*starosta*). This position is usually staffed by a boy in his late teens, or by a widow or a soldier's wife. Women arrive first and start the singing. Then the men arrive and treat them to vodka and other refreshments they have brought, consisting usually of honey cakes, sunflower seeds, apples, sugar candies, and pretzels.

The company alternately sings, drinks, eats, dances, and plays the card game "War," and group games with names such as "Monks," "Neighbors," and "Cossacks." Essentially all these games amount to kissing. For example, in "Neighbors" the elder places men and women on benches in pairs at his own discretion, then approaches each pair and inquires whether they are happy with each other's company. If, for example, the girl does not like her "neighbor," she can request someone else's company. The elder then says: "Since you are satisfied with one another, mow two oat fields for me," or "measure me eight yards of lace" (meaning two or eight kisses). In the game "Monks," men take turns leaving the room and knocking on the door. When the elder opens the door, the caller says: "Father Superior! Give me a nun!" whereupon the elder asks which nun is desired. The man whispers the name of a particular young woman. The elder then brings him the woman, and the two retire to the hallway for a brief kissing session.

Sometimes the parties break up violently. The young men drink too much and begin fighting, smashing window panes and dishes as well. Occasionally the hostess, too, gets beaten up.

The other day I heard a song that startled me. In a few words, it portrays everything that I gathered from my own observations and inquiries. I offer the story here as a very characteristic representation of village mores. It is a dance tune played at street parties:

Don't delay, young woman,
Have fun while you may.
In the autumn you'll be given away in marriage
And won't enjoy such freedom anymore.
My worthless husband will climb on top of me
And abuse me.
He'll get up and abuse me some more
And will swear at me and scorn me.
Aren't you a dandy, Ivan,
I loved you,
And hid you out
Behind the tool rack back of the oven,
So that the old man wouldn't know,
And would not go searching for you.
But he went looking around the closets,
And found you by the oven,
By the oven, behind the tool rack,
And grabbed you by the shoulders.
The cute little guy pined away,
What with no one to make love to:
To make love to a married woman—
You have to give her gold,
Make love to a soldier's wife—
And she could get killed,
But to make it with a pretty maiden,
You have to play the dandy.

According to my observations, the young men who are most successful with the women are those who are "neatly dressed," i.e., have a waistcoat, a jacket, top boots, and a nice peaked cap. They can also make a favorable impression by skillfully playing the accordion, by using certain polite or playful expressions (nowadays every girl at the street parties is addressed as "miss"), and perhaps by a display of ready wit. Previously, the dress of the young men was not as important as it has become. The young women liked curly-headed, rosy-complexioned, easy-going boys, and did not mind that they wore bast shoes. [Nowadays] men still are outfitted for everyday wear with clothes made at home: shirts, trousers, foot cloths, bast shoes, peasant vests (*poddyovki*), sheepskin coats. But on holidays, the men, especially the young ones, wear cotton shirts, trousers of lasting cloth, waistcoats (*zhiletki*) (sometimes even a jacket and galoshes), and tapered top boots. Felt boots (*valenki*) are home-made.

The most successful girls at the street gatherings are those who are cheerful and outgoing, and who can dance well. In the opinion of one landowner, the more indecently a girl behaves at the parties, the greater success she enjoys. Now, however, every girl has a special boyfriend whom she "loves" or "hangs out with," and she waits for him to pick her out at the country dances. He gives her presents such as a cotton kerchief, a cheap ring or earrings, or a bar of aromatic soap, and he may treat her to sunflowers, honey cakes, or rolls. Girls, too, sometimes give treats to their boyfriends (usually when they walk them home after the party) or sew them a tobacco pouch from scraps of cloth. Remarkably, it is the women who walk their boyfriends home, and not the other way around. A boy will not even see his girlfriend to the doorstep, but the girls walk their partners home, whether they are boyfriends or fiancés. This curious behavior is even mentioned in the peasants' songs.

Professional prostitution does not exist, but it is easy to purchase a woman with money or gifts. One woman naively confided: "I was stupid enough to end up with a son for a trifle—a dozen apples." Women and girls enjoy getting apples from the leased orchards. They barter eggs for the apples, and occasionally they barter their own bodies.

There was a case this summer in which a twenty-year-old guard at the apple orchard raped a thirteen-year-old girl. The mother of the girl—a very poor woman, it is true—agreed to forgive the offender in exchange for three rubles. The poor girl wailed for two or three days after the incident, and what a terrified and tormented look she had! Witnesses to the rape were girls of the same age who had stumbled into the guard's tent at the very moment he was raping the girl and holding his hand over her mouth. Later the girl reported that when the youth began to rape her, he said: "Don't be afraid, you won't get pregnant; only grownup women get pregnant." And when she wanted to scream, he said: "Don't scream, girl, and I'll give you a ruble."

Sometimes in the spring, before the field-work season starts, a number of women, married and unmarried, from the same village set out on a pilgrimage to Voronezh or to the Trinity monastery. Parents and husbands know very well what kind of pilgrimage the women have in mind, but women who have agreed among themselves represent a force that is difficult to resist. They go from one village to another appealing for night lodgings in the name of Christ, and anything and everything happens at these overnight stays. One peasant justly referred to the pilgrimage as "a service for a dark god [*chernobog*]."

Abortions are fairly frequent. The wife of a local landlord used to help women in difficult labor, giving them a brew of "cossack juniper" (*Juniperus sabina*), which grew abundantly in her garden and was believed to accelerate labor. Ever since the villagers discovered the properties of the plant, "invisible hands" (in the landlord's words) regularly pluck the juniper bushes at night, apparently for use as an abortifacient; the landlord never refuses to give the brew from the plant to a laboring woman.

Cases of infanticide of illegitimate babies are not at all rare. A married or unmarried woman gives birth alone somewhere in a shed, smothers the baby, and dumps it into the river (with a rock secured to its neck) or leaves it in a hemp thicket, or buries it either in the yard or somewhere in the pigpen. Once a widow gave birth on the eve of Easter when everyone was in church, and she smothered the baby, thinking [as she later explained] "it would kick the bucket[3] from hunger in any case." (The woman had six children, not counting the baby.) She took it to the shed where she kept her trunk and locked it in the trunk, for she expected everyone to return soon from church. All day Easter Sunday she stayed in bed, telling people that she felt very ill. At night when everyone

3. The woman uses the word *okolet'*, which is normally used to describe the death of an animal.

A group of peasant women. Courtesy of the Library of Congress.

was asleep, she picked up a pail (as if she were going to get water) and went to the shed, where she removed the body from the trunk. Placing it in the pail, she rushed to the pond and disposed of her cargo (weighed down with a rock). Afterwards she returned home with an innocent-looking pail of water. In the morning she left the house altogether and found work elsewhere as a cook. The child was discovered a month later when the pond went dry, and the widow was found out.

Another time a girl was caught when a dog dragged from a hemp field the body of a smothered baby that she had hidden there. In fact, in the large village of Muraevnia, one or two children are found dead almost every year. But only rarely are the mothers identified. Recently, pigs rooted out by the graveyard the body of a newborn that had turned blue, making it obvious that the baby had been buried a very short time before. No action was taken in the matter. Peasants do not like criminal investigations and keep quiet even when they know something. The priest, too, has a similar attitude toward these matters. "It is a sin, but only God knows who did it. Another person's soul is impenetrable; how are you going to find out? There are plenty of girls carousing." Sometimes illegitimate children are taken to the foundling home in Moscow.[4] Muraevnia even has a woman who, for a small price, transports these "good-time children" to the foundling home. Once a woman went to a childless local landlord with a proposal that he purchase her newborn baby. "I heard that you need a child. Well, I thought you could buy this one. He is a 'good-time baby,' and my husband will be coming home soon."

There are a number of reasons why morals are more relaxed now than they were in earlier times. First, people are more apt nowadays to work away from home, and interactions with other villages are more regular and frequent. Previously, village life was self-contained. The villagers worked exclusively for their owner. Now, in contrast, peasants from different villages meet at the estates of various landlords where they have hired on as day laborers. A girl can sign up for day labor wherever she likes and thus escape the supervision of her home community.

At the same time, a new practice has begun; in contrast to earlier times, young men now can go to the country dances at any village they like. Moreover, farm laborers from nearby estates descend uninvited on the local village, adding still another foreign element to the village street gatherings. (Women and girls never go to another village for street parties.) These men can woo the

4. For a detailed description and analysis of the foundling homes and the peasants' use of them, see my book *Mothers of Misery: Child Abandonment in Russia* (Princeton: Princeton University Press, 1988).

local girls with complete impunity; since they are outsiders, there is no way to restrain them. If a village girl takes up with a landowner's farm laborer, the affair is bound to be very short-lived, for the landowner tries to hire the workers from a distant village, fifteen to thirty kilometers away, and her man will leave as soon as his contract expires. For a woman, too, it is safer to be involved with a farm laborer who is here today and gone tomorrow, than with someone from her own village; this way she avoids gossip.

The relaxation of morals is also facilitated by the absence of husbands off on migrant labor. The man acquires a mistress, while his wife may carry on an affair back home. If childless, she may in her husband's absence hire on as a cook for the workers at the landlord's estate. If she has a child, she will visit for several weeks at her mother's, who of course will "cover for" her daughter under any circumstances. As the saying goes, "When the cat's away, the mice will play."[5]

An unmarried girl will not always ask for money in return for sexual relations. But virtually every grown woman will demand payment, and some will even ask for payment in advance. Women do not sin "for free," unless it is some utterly cowed and timid widow. [Of course, not all widows are cowed and timid.] Some arrange things for themselves quite nicely. In our village, there is one widow who took in a son-in-law by marrying off her simple-minded, browbeaten eighteen-year-old daughter, and the widow shares the man with her daughter. When the son-in-law gets drunk, fights break out in this *ménage à trois,* but everything ends well, and the woman lives much better with her son-in-law than she did with her weak, sickly husband. She is the envy of many women in the village.

"Wayward women," a term applied to maidens or married women who have several lovers, are sometimes punished. The lovers may decide to get together and teach their sweetheart a lesson. If she is unmarried, they spread tar on the gate to her

5. Literally, "Hide and seek and other games brought the gal to Johnny."

house. A married woman is beaten, and, with her dress hoisted and fastened sacklike around her head and her body exposed from the waist down, she is paraded through the village. A girl that has only one lover is not nowadays considered "wayward" and is spared having her gate tarred.

The following event, which occurred in a remote village, illustrates the mores. The parents of a young woman who had gotten pregnant out of wedlock married her off to hide her sin. When the woman gave birth, her husband's family [with whom she was then living] turned against the child. Although her husband was a peaceful, simple-hearted fellow who did not reproach his wife for her youthful indiscretion, his family was relentless and eventually demanded that she "get rid of the little bastard." This demand was so insistent, the poor woman being continually beaten and persecuted by her in-laws, that she gave in. She filled the infant's pacifier rag with sulfur scraped off matches, placed it in the baby's mouth, and it soon died. The mother was taken to court but was acquitted.

5

❖❖❖

IVAN PREPARES FOR MARRIAGE

Another realm in which women played a central role was the arrangement of marriages. In theory, the timing of marriage, the choice of partners, and the content of the ceremony and accompanying celebrations were almost entirely in the hands of women. This amounted to power over the establishment of kinship bonds, an altogether critical function in peasant society, one on which the survival of the family could ultimately depend. Semyonova states this view of things at the start of this chapter, but the stories she tells later show young men proposing to women; the role of the women of the young man's household is not presented. At the end of the chapter, I have inserted unpublished descriptions of four actual marriages taken from Semyonova's field notes. While women clearly played a directing role in the last two cases, their influence in the first two instances is less obviously determining.

Semyonova dwells on the age of marriage partners and suggests that Russian ideas about the appropriate age difference between them may reflect a mechanism of natural selection. These comments should be seen in the context of the powerful influence of Darwinian thought at the time Semyonova was growing up and writing. Scholars now understand such behavior as a product of an interaction of economy and culture. In this connection, it is interesting to note that Russian practices shared one key element with the rather unusual patterns of northwestern Europe (where people tended to marry late, the age gaps between bride and groom were small, and many people never married) and had other elements in common with the customs of southern Europe and much of Asia (where people married early, grooms were significantly older than brides, and nearly everyone married). In peasant Russia, marriage occurred early and was virtually universal, but as in western Europe, Russian couples were very close in age; often the bride was older than her groom.

❖

WHEN THE TIME COMES for the young man Ivan to consider marrying, discussion of the matter in the family amounts to calculating the possible benefits. A man must get married if he is to become a genuine *muzhik,* which is to say a fully responsible adult male or *zhitel'* (literally, resident). The groom's parents see his future wife as labor power that they are eager to obtain.

It is usually the women, not the men, who first broach the subject of marriage. The men's role is merely to assent to what the women agree on. A married daughter might say to her mother: "It's time, Mother, that you got someone to relieve you in the house," or "at the hearth." "So it is," replies the mother, "but Grishka is involved with Dunka Vinokurova, that good-for-nothing, and her father would be happy to coax Grishka into being his son-in-law before we know it. I am afraid even to mention the subject to Grishka. He has eyes for no one but Dunka." A "good-for-nothing" is a young woman who spins poorly, weaves badly, and is no good at field work. Some young women are "bad-tempered" and "stubborn," others are "cunning," and a third type is "promiscuous," "tarts." Still others are "sickly." "She's a good girl but is sick all the time. She never has any color in her face. And her eyes are always watery."

A young woman should be "intelligent, healthy, handy, reserved, and ready to do any kind of work." It happens, however, that fifteen to twenty-five rubles[1] given by the woman's father will make up for the lack of health, intelligence, or good behavior. The parents of the groom fall for this "compensation" all too readily. The grooms themselves never get to see this type of cash dowry. One man was indignant about the wife of his brother. "We married him off, all right, but his wife is worthless—she can't spin or sew. You know as well as I do why our brother married: for a shirt and a pair of pants."

The notion of beauty is very elementary. Local women are certainly pretty, tall and, at the age of fifteen or sixteen, well formed, even though after that age their figures become misshapen from hard work. The earlier a woman marries, the sooner she takes on a withered and emaciated appearance. The most common type here are dark-complexioned women with proportional features, dark gray eyes, which are strikingly beautiful in some cases, dark eyebrows, and dark hair; there are virtually no true blonds. More often you find brunettes with dark eyes.

What we would regard as the most beautiful women are not considered as such by the peasants. In the choice of a bride or a girlfriend, peasant taste does not correspond to ours. We prefer straight, clean lines and features, while a peasant is all for a plump, heavy-set girl or woman. Pallid faces are very unpopular, as is a "solemn" expression: the peasants regard these as signs of sullenness, unsociability, or stupidity. A woman's face should be open and cheerful. Black eyebrows will win many a heart. A man should have curly hair and, again, black eyebrows. Height is an important asset for both sexes. "Full-bodied girl, robust, black brows, rosy-cheeked, radiant eyes"—all these are compliments for a woman. Red-haired people are disliked, probably because of some [magical] characteristics ascribed to them in past times, traits that would have had purportedly harmful effects on one's household. My inquiries have led me to the conclusion that redheads are still regarded secretly as perfidious and evil.

1. The equivalent of a half-year's earnings for many peasants.

Peasant women from Riazan province, selected for appearance and dress typical of the region. Photo by I. P. Semyonov from *Rossiia. Polnoe geograficheskoe opisanie*, vol. 2, p. 188.

Incidentally, the choice of a mate is frequently more a matter of circumstance (*sluchainost'*) than of taste, for which there sometimes is no allowance at all; some of the men are remarkably undemanding in this regard. Men who have lived in town are no more demanding than those who stay at home. Frequently the opposite is the case. To say that all peasants are undiscriminating would not be true, yet really choosy young men are quite rare. A "good-looking eligible woman" ("good-looking" according to primitive peasant tastes, of course) has more suitors than a plain one, but a man who gets turned down by a beautiful woman is not at all embarrassed to marry the most homely one. As for the groom's parents, they are solely concerned about the bride's ability and willingness to work, although in recent years the cash dowry has taken on increasing importance in the choice the in-laws must make.

The peasants believe that it is best for a couple to be of the same age. Young women are very reluctant to marry men a few years older than they are. Why this is, God only knows. It could have to do with fears of the men being closer to death, for brides who are four or five years younger than their grooms have complained that "he is going to die before I do." Probably this is just one cause. The attitude may also go back to some ancient tradition which prescribes that spouses be of the same age. It could be that in the distant past, a form of natural selection was involved. In any event, to this day brides in our area are mortally offended by the prospect of having to marry a man six or eight years older. They weep and wail when forced by their parents to marry a man so much older, and their girlfriends make fun of them for having to do so. Yet men of eighteen to twenty have no misgivings about marrying women two or even four years older than they. I can recall two weddings last fall (the only two weddings that took place in our township, as it happened) when eighteen- and twenty-year-old men married women of twenty and twenty-six respectively. In fact, wives are often older than their husbands. This year eight weddings took place in our village of twenty-five to thirty households; in one of these the groom was eighteen years old and the bride twenty-four, in another the groom was twenty and the bride twenty-five. Wives in four other couples I know in the same village are from two to seven years older than their husbands. As for the age gap in older couples, it is simply lost in the sands of time. These notions [about the age of brides] belong to young men and women who have not lived in town; young "Ivans" who have been drawn into the orbit of town life and manners may view these age gaps differently.[2]

In relations between young people, the earlier peasant notion that a gift has to be reciprocated has not been completely abandoned, and the whole business is not yet reduced to a question of money, as in the case of payments for sex. Some semblance of love remains. A girl will sew a shirt for the boy she loves if he asks her to; a boy will be pleased to see his girlfriend wearing a kerchief or a ring that he has given her. In general, a boy expresses his love for a girl in gifts, kind words, and kisses. But once a woman becomes a wife, even right after the wedding, her husband treats her as his personal property and sees no reason to caress her and kiss her, let alone give her a gift. It is good enough if a young husband refrains from beating his wife or allowing his family at the very beginning to pile too much work on her.

The manner in which a young man makes a marriage proposal varies according to the circumstances. After a series of meetings at country dances, parties, and games, when a young man finally gets to be alone with the young woman he likes, he asks: "Will you marry me?" More often than not the girl first exclaims: "Where on earth did you get such an idea!" giggling and covering her face with a kerchief or turning away from the boy. She may inform her wooer that arrangements are under way to marry her to someone else, or she could make some other excuse or delaying tactic.

"Don't beat around the bush," her sweetheart presses her. "Tell me straight: will you marry me or not? If so, I will send a matchmaker for you."

2. This paragraph was woven together from comments widely separated in the published text (from pages 53-54 and 72). See additional examples of this reaction to age differences in the descriptions of actual marriages below.

Eventually, if she likes the fellow, the girl will reply very softly: "I will."

"That's the way! I do like you, Annushka, and to you alone will I propose, to no one but you." This may be followed by a kiss, which Annushka will surely try to avoid. This exchange takes place in a corner of the yard, behind a barn, or in the hayricks. Before they depart, the couple agree on the time the boy will send a matchmaker for his betrothed.

If the two are already having relations, the procedure is slightly different. After a sexual encounter somewhere under a haystack or in the ricks, the boy will say: "Well, Matryona, I guess I will officially propose to you. I think my family will be happy to have you. You're a fine gal, all right!"

Matryona will reply: "It surely would be nice to go to the altar. And it would be a sin not to. I didn't spare myself for you, although it's not easy. You talked me into this by promising to marry me. . . . Now if I get pregnant, what am I going to do? I might as well tie a stone around my neck and throw myself into the river!" By now, her eyes will be brimming with tears.

The boy: "Now, now, don't cry. Do you think I am rejecting you? I am going to talk with my father and mother and then send the matchmaker for you."

Matryona: "Well, Vania, I am looking forward to it."

[What Semyonova calls "coaxing" or a kind of sexual bargaining is another aspect of the courting relationship, which is illustrated by this next report.]

In a recess under a hayloft, a couple is seated. The boy attempts to embrace the girl.

Matryona: "Stop it! Don't touch me; leave me alone or I'll scream!"

Ivan: "Silly, I won't hurt you . . . ," and in agitation he takes hold of the girl's dress. "Matryonushka, let's have fun, honey, I beg you! (Ever more agitated) Just wait and see what a shawl I am going to buy you! And I'll propose to you, too. I'm not fit to live if I don't marry you!"

Matryona, making an attempt to recover her hem, almost cries: "Look here, now, let me go, stop it, don't sin!"

Ivan: "How can it be a sin if we are going to be married?" Eventually he manages to embrace the girl.

Matryona, resignedly: "This is scary!"

[Here follow descriptions of actual marriages.][3]

This fall we had four weddings in the village. A twenty-six-year-old woman by the name of Zinaida was married off to a twenty-two-year-old fellow in a neighboring village.[4] Zinaida's family is not wealthy. She has an aging father, sixty-four years old, a mother, and a sister seventeen years of age. Their farming operation is middling; the livestock consist of one horse, a pig, a piglet, and three sheep. The father is still strong and without great effort manages to farm his land allotment of about seven acres. Zinaida herself has long been known in these parts as a splendid worker. "She can do the work of three men," the people say. She is quite a handsome woman, tall, plump, with reddish hair, gray eyes, the kind of pug nose that is favored here, and a large mouth. In the winter she turns very pale, but in the summer her face is covered with freckles. You could say that she remained unmarried to good account, "building up her strength." Zinaida also has a good personality; she is cheerful, works without complaining, and is not a mischief-maker—"she has no duplicity about her whatever." Some rumors went around about her having had relations with one young fellow, and as a result of that and the fact that her father valued her as a worker, she remained unmarried until age twenty-six. Her "beau" is from an average family. He has a mother, two young sisters, and three brothers. His name is Yakov Danilin, and he is an attractive young man. Both the bride and the groom look very happy, and people remark that "they are truly very satisfied with one another." In a year or so, the couple will move from the young man's home to the home of Zinaida's father. Yakov and his brothers are going to divide the family property among themselves, and Yakov will

3. Taken from an unpublished typescript in Semyonova's archive. AGO, f. 109, op. 1, d. 170, ch. 4, ll. 1-4.

4. This age arrangement does not fit with any of the marriages Semyonova mentioned earlier in this chapter. But keep in mind that she collected material over a four-year period, and this report may have been made in another year.

then move over to become heir to the household of his father-in-law, Nikita Openkin.[5]

The next two young people to get married are from well-to-do families. The younger son of Adrian Ushakov, "Iliushka," age nineteen, is marrying a woman of approximately the same age from a neighboring village. Iliushka is tall, sensible, and generally a spirited lad. His young wife is a tall, fair-skinned blond who is a "seamstress," that is to say she has worked for several years in cottage industry, embroidery in particular, which is a specialty of the village of Muraevnia among peasants with small land allotments. She dresses "chic," as they say here, wearing a wool sarafan trimmed in silk and a black silk blouse with a lace bodice; her head is covered by a colorful cashmere shawl, and she adorns herself with silver earrings, finger rings, and so forth. Of course, you would never see a woman like this doing field work. But Adrian's two other sons (who still live at home) are already married to robust, simple peasant women, good workers, and for this reason the parents did not seek out the kind of woman who could "take charge." Iliushka himself picked out his bride, and eventually he will go off with her to Moscow. This couple, too, look very satisfied with their match.

The third wedding saw an old woman, Tatiana Voronina, give away her granddaughter "Alyonka." Tatiana is sixty-six years old and the wife of Kharlan Seleznyov. Although his last name is Seleznyov, his wife is referred to as Tatiana Voronina after her father, who was nicknamed "Vorona," that is, "crow." Everyone says Kharlan Seleznyov, but only rarely does anyone say Tatiana Seleznyova; everyone calls her Voronina. Perhaps it is thanks to her unmistakable individuality that people find it hard to refer to her by her husband's name. Tatiana is a tough old lady with straight features and extremely animated and sly gray eyes. Her

5. Here we see a common Russian practice in families that do not produce surviving male offspring to take over the parents' farming operation. A daughter is married to a young man who cannot count on inheriting much from his own family, and the son-in-law (known in this case as *priemysh*) is brought into his bride's home as the prospective household head.

face is pale and wrinkled, but she holds her head erect, and her movements are quick, not those of an elderly person. Her "Kharlan" is a homely old fellow, hunched over, but still boasting completely black hair. His voice is weak, and his facial features are nondescript. He is attached to her, and she runs the entire household. Tatiana is both a folk healer and a village midwife. She is the mother of six sons and three daughters. Four of her sons are married, and one of these has already moved out and established his own household because of his wife's inability to get along with other people. All three daughters have, as they say, "been distributed," that is, given away in matrimony; one son had to go off to the army, and the youngest boy, her "heir," Fediushka, is only fourteen.

Her granddaughter Alyonka is eighteen years of age. Tatiana sought out for her in a neighboring village a thirty-year-old man who had just returned from St. Petersburg, where he spent three years working in a weapons factory. He earned a good wage there, and rumor has it that he was able to put three hundred rubles in the bank. He came home at the insistence of his parents, who wanted him to get married, and when he took an immediate liking to Alyonka Voronina,[6] Tatiana was quick to take advantage of the circumstance. Alyonka's mother was a docile woman completely under the thumb of her mother-in-law, and although she felt terrible about having to part with her only daughter, she was incapable of putting up a fight against Tatiana; she merely went into fainting spells when she had to give her parental blessing to Alyonka, and she passed out completely when her daughter left for the church. Alyonka herself felt awful about having to marry an "old man," a person not of her age group. The entire week prior to the wedding she was not herself; she wore herself to a frazzle with grief, wailing lamentations, but she, too, did not dare to thwart her grandmother's will (her father played a rather un-

6. If this transcription in the archival file is accurate, it reveals the power of the Voronin name to eclipse the legal family name of Seleznyov right down to the third generation.

concerned and passive role in all this). For some time after the engagement, Alyonka kept her "young man"[7] at a distance, pushed him away, even told him he could "go to hell" and said she "had no need of him." He tried to entice her with promises of taking her to "Piter"[8] and buying her fancy outfits and the like. "To hell with your 'Piter' and your fine outfits, for all I care. I don't need them," she would respond.

I saw the couple on the day after the wedding. The young, tall, ruddy girl with her not especially intelligent face made an effort to "hold her mug" away from her husband, but it was clear that talk of St. Petersburg and "fancy outfits" was finally having some effect, and that Alyonka was outgrowing the traditional village notions about the "disgrace" attached to marrying an older man. A week later, the pair visited me in the company of the grandmother, and you should have seen the courtesy with which the "young man" (not for nothing had he lived in St. Petersburg) handed his "grandmother" her overcoat and helped her into it. "There, you see what honor I have attained," the old woman joked with self-satisfaction. And Alyonka had become far less distant to her husband. "What a woman Grandma Tania is!" [she remarked].

How much such a woman can mean for a peasant family! "She built her entire house," people say, and in her time gave birth to twelve children, nine of which survived. When the children were young, she went out begging to get enough to feed them; later she became a folk healer and midwife—and at one time she even ran an "underground tavern" [selling bootleg liquor]. There was nothing she would not do in order to see that her children survived and got on their feet. "Grandma Tania is never wrong," they all say. The only person I felt sorry for in the whole business was Alyonka's mother.

At the fourth wedding, Tikhon Marsakov was to give away his son Grishka. Tikhon was a quiet, hardworking old man of average

7. Here is an untranslatable play on the Russian word *molodoi,* which can mean both "young" and "bridegroom." "Young man" seems best to catch the irony, which was clearly intended.
8. St. Petersburg.

means, a widower. In actuality, Grishka was being married off not by him but by his married sister and sister-in-law. Grishka is a tall, hearty fellow, but childish and not good-looking. He has already finished his military service. They found him a young woman in a neighboring village, an orphan of about twenty years of age who to our way of thinking is extraordinarily attractive. Grishka at first had no objection to her, and the engagement took place in the usual manner. This happened in September. After the engagement, however, another young woman began "pushing herself upon" Grishka, a forward and unattractive woman from his own village. She convinced her father and mother that it was time for her to get married, that it was a good harvest year, and that she liked Grishka. So they set out to "foist" her on Grishka. And it turned out that Grishka liked her, God only knows why (perhaps they had "fallen in love" during the fall parties). Whatever the case may have been, a week before the planned wedding, Grishka began to reject his betrothed. And then the whole family started in on him—his father, brothers, and sisters-in-law: "You can't back out of this now after the engagement and everything has been agreed upon; we aren't in a position to pay the penalties for this," and so on and so forth. On the eve of the wedding, Grishka broke all the dishes in his father's house, saying, "Just as I don't want these dishes, I don't want my bride-to-be." The noise and screaming were deafening, and the women squealed and took cover under the benches, but they nevertheless insisted on having their way and . . . [the manuscript breaks off at this point, but it seems that Grishka was going to have to bow to the will of his family after all. It would have been remarkable had he been able to stand up to their collective opposition.]

6

❖❖❖

PLEDGING THE BRIDE, THE BRIDE-SHOW, AND MARRIAGE

Once a young couple or the family of an eligible man decided to initiate an official proposal of marriage, one or more matchmakers had to be engaged to make the initial approaches to the family of the bride-to-be. Assuming everyone agreed, the pledging was then followed by a bride-show, and finally the official church marriage ceremony. Some scholars believe that the betrothal (or the betrothal and bride-show together) represented the pre-Christian rites, and these rites sealed the marriage from the peasant point of view ("the wine is drunk"), for the couple at that point could begin sexual relations. This view strikes me as romanticized, for the essence of the bargain was the transfer of the bride to a new household, and this did not occur until after the church ceremony. The marriage bond clearly required all three steps in order to enjoy the sanction of the village community.

Semyonova's account raises some additional difficulties in this regard, because of the stress the older generation, at least, appears to have placed on the bride's virginity. Remarks in this chapter and elsewhere in this study make clear that young people no longer seemed to attach a high value to premarital celibacy.

Weddings in this community normally took place during the week-long festival of St. Michael in the fall following the harvest. I have placed a reckoning of expenditures of three families of different means at the end of the chapter (the reckonings are from Semyonova's unpublished notes), followed by stories about two other marriages, which Semyonova reported in the form of dialogue.

MATCHMAKING SERVICES are not entrusted to outsiders. Usually the matchmaker is a female relative experienced in such matters. She cannot be considered a specialist for the village as a whole, since she provides this service only to her own kin. In general, relatives and the respect paid to them play an enormous role in all "solemn occasions" of peasant life, such as weddings, baptisms, and funerals. (Outsiders are invited to funeral dinners, however, for they offer prayers for the deceased and thus facilitate his entry into heaven. This belief is associated with the notion of the ordeals of the soul after death.)

The mother of the groom, accompanied by his grandmother, aunt, or godmother, comes to the prospective bride's house to propose. They exchange greetings with the bride's mother, who probably already knows the purpose of their visit and is waiting for them in the house. The visitors look at the ceiling beam and announce, "We need to cross beyond that beam," which means they want to propose to the bride.

"Well, it's a good thing to do."

"You have a daughter, and we have a son."

"Well, good luck!"

"We are not joking."

"Neither am I. I have no objection, but I have to ask her father."

The father is sent for. After a consultation in the hallway, he is brought in to the matchmakers. The earlier conversation is repeated, the visitors standing by the door all the while. [Finally the bride's parents say,] "We have no objections. Now we must ask our daughter." The daughter is sent for (meanwhile she has changed into a cleaner sarafan and a kerchief). In the hallway she is asked whether she wants to marry the man. She replies: "Let it be as you, father and mother, would wish it." She is brought in, and the visitors have a good look at her. Her parents say: "Now we can drink on it." A bottle of vodka and other refreshments are placed on the table. The visitors also produce a bottle and some food that they have brought with them. The young woman leaves the room. The two parties to the transaction sit down at the table, drink, eat, and discuss the gifts to be exchanged between the bride and the groom. If the bride's parents do not want to marry their daughter off on this occasion, they will demand an unreasonable brideprice. If the proposing party did not like the prospective bride, they will not even sit down to drink, but right after the bride leaves the room, they excuse themselves, explaining that they need to give the matter more thought and to discuss it with the rest of the family and with the groom. After the brideprice and the gifts have been agreed upon and the wine is drunk, the girl is considered "pledged."

The rules governing the behavior of a betrothed couple in intimate relations prior to marriage [differ from those for couples that are merely dating]. The couple act upon the belief that since "the wine was drunk," which is to say that they received their blessing at the engagement and the families have, moreover, incurred expenses, the matter cannot possibly fall through. All things considered, the young woman feels confident yielding to her betrothed if an opportunity is offered by a late party, a warm night, or a happy moment when the couple can inconspicuously slip off to a barn or vacant house.

Sometimes a betrothed young man will renounce his promised one after the engagement, or, as happens more often, the young woman will renounce him, because he is frequently the choice of her parents, not her, and she may get cold feet at the last minute. In these cases, the offended family claims restitution. The penalty imposed on the family committing the breach of promise is anywhere from ten to twenty-five rubles and is legally enforced through a judgment handed down by the village council (*mirskii prigovor*).

In some villages, a potential bride [who has not been sued for by the usual age] is presented publicly for marrying. She is dressed up, and her father or another male relative drives her through her home village as well as through some of the neighboring villages. The wagon rolls slowly through the village, and the girl's father cries out: "Anyone need a stone post?" Everybody gathers to look at the bride, and if someone likes the looks of her, he will invite her to his house with the words: "A pipe, a pipe! Turn in here!" The woman and her father or brother enter the house, and she is given a closer inspection. If the man in question still likes what he sees, a date for the pledging ceremony will be set.

One or two weeks after the proposal, the bride-show is scheduled. The groom's family provides refreshments (pancakes, fried chicken, pie, pickles, honey cakes, pretzels, sunflower seeds, vodka). All these are placed in a trunk, and the groom and his family take it to the bride's house. They enter the house, and the men together with the groom take one bench, while the women from the groom's side sit down on another bench nearby. The trunk with the refreshments is placed by the stove. The bride meanwhile puts on her best clothes and is led into the room by her married sister or sister-in-law. The bride bows to the groom and his family and greets each woman with a kiss. The groom and his family rise. The bride is now standing in front of the groom. Her head kerchief is tied in such a way that her face is shaded. The groom's family inspects the bride closely. "Perhaps she is lame?" they may inquire. Her sister or sister-in-law then has her walk around the room. Other questions are asked, for example, about whether she may be deaf. Then her future parents-in-law approach the bride and ask: "Why is she wrapped like that so we can't see her eyes; is she possibly blind in one eye?" The bride's sister uncovers her face for inspection. If the bride is pale, the groom's family will want to know the reason, asking whether she is sickly.

The following day the groom may come in a cart to take the bride and her girlfriends for a ride. He then takes them to a tavern, where he treats them to tea, honey cakes, and occasionally vodka. During the ride, the girls honor the couple with songs and beat on scythes for accompaniment. The horse is usually adorned with bells and pieces of cloth woven into its mane. If the groom's parents like the bride, his mother ties around the bride's head a kerchief that is brought for the occasion, while his father places a coin (sometimes even one ruble) on the top of her head. After this, the groom's parents take their son aside, while the bride's parents do the same with their daughter. The groom is asked whether he likes the bride, and she is asked a similar question. If they are to each other's liking, the answer is: "If you, father and mother, like him/her, so do I." After this the groom and the bride stand next to each other, and their relatives perform a blessing with an icon: first the parents of the groom, then the parents of the bride, followed by their respective godparents. The couple bow deeply to them and kiss the icon. Then the couple go hand in hand to the other house (if the family has a second dwelling on its property) or to a neighbor's. There a table is already set for them.

During this procession, the groom has the right to examine his bride's body by touch, especially if it seems to him that she has a physical defect. A skinny bride, foreseeing this, will pad herself with a large number of skirts and sarafans to appear pudgier. If the groom discovers that the bride is pregnant, he may go back to his parents and call off the wedding, although this rarely happens; some men will intentionally go for a "good-time" girl who has a substantial dowry, while others are too timid to examine their brides thoroughly. Since bride-shows normally take place in late fall and frequently in the evening, it is easy for the groom to check over the bride by taking her into the unlit hall or outdoors, either on the road in front of the house or even into the dark backyard. The bride is supposed to keep quiet during the inspection and obey her husband-to-be.

When they come back into the house, the groom's brother seats them at the table in the place of honor (the corner to the left of the entrance door under the icon [known to Russians as the "holy" or "beautiful" corner]). Then the bride's girlfriends arrive and sit at the table. First the groom's treats and vodka are served. The couple drink first, and the girls follow. After all of this has been consumed, the bride's brother places the bride's treats on the table, and the same order of drinking and eating is repeated. The girls sing songs for the occasion and then start dancing. Very often they become drunk. The groom and the bride sit next to each other and eat honey cakes or crack sunflower seeds. They are allowed to squeeze one another's hand and converse. When everything has been eaten and all the songs have been sung, the couple, again holding hands, proceed to the house where earlier the bride was first presented. During this move, the groom has another opportunity to examine his bride by touch. Onc woman, who married off her son to a very poor girl favored by the boy, teased her son that his wife had a mutilated finger (her finger had been smashed in a door when she was a child). The son replied: "Well, mother, I examined her all right but couldn't make out that anything was wrong with her finger, and indeed you yourself failed to notice anything when Tania was officially presented."

In the first house, the in-laws, and for that matter all the older people, have been celebrating ever since the bride left. There too the couple are given the place of honor, and their elders drink to their health and toast them. Then the bride rises and presents gifts to her in-laws: a shirt for her father-in-law, a kerchief for her mother-in-law, and towels for other relatives. After this the groom's family rides off in carts, while he walks home, again holding hands with his bride, who accompanies him to the end of the village or to the nearest street corner. The bride's girlfriends follow along and again accompany the couple with singing. At this point it is already very late at night, and if the groom did not find an opportunity to examine his bride earlier when they were walking from one house to the other, this is the time to do it. At the end of the village the procession stops. The groom kisses his bride and treats her to honey cakes, sunflower seeds, and apples.

The bride then returns home. She tears off the ceremonial kerchief and pounds her head on a bench while crying out a lamentation or, as it is known here, "the scream." Her mother and sister join in:

> My father, my provider,
> My dearest mother,
> I've been given away, miserable and hapless,
> And giving me away they washed it down with vodka
> And a burnt bread crust.
> How will it turn out for me going to live with strangers,
> To a new father and mother.
> I will have to please these strangers,
> To be pleasing and obedient to them all.

After this, everyone retires for the night. The bride shouts out this lament every evening of the week preceding the wedding. Some brides are completely hoarse by the time they go to church to be wed.

Between the bride-show and the wedding, the groom may call upon his bride several times. On these occasions he brings vodka and treats his prospective relatives. He also brings treats for the bride. When the groom leaves for home, the bride walks him to a street corner. At this point in their relationship, the couple are likely to begin having sex.

On the eve of the wedding, a party for the bride's girlfriends is held.[1] On the afternoon of the day of the party, the parents of the groom arrive to collect the bride's gifts for him. On his behalf, they present her with a pound of soap and a pair of earrings. Soon the girlfriends arrive. The bride serves them refreshments and vodka. The girls honor her with songs. Then the bride addresses her parents with a lamentation:

> My father, my provider,
> My dearest mother,
> Thank you for your hospitality.
> My stay with you has ended,

1. The party is referred to in Russian as the *devichnik*.

Young women participating in the *devichnik*, or party for the bride's girlfriends on the eve of the wedding. Two of the women carry the lace and embroidered cloth which Russian village women were skilled at making and which were used as gifts and as part of the trousseau. Village of Kharlampievskaia, Riazan province. Courtesy of the Riazan Museum.

And the festivities are over for me—
This is my very last day,
This is my very last hour.

After this the bride undresses, and her closest friend gives her a steam bath inside the stove, washing her with the groom's soap. The girls sing:

Burn red-hot, new bath,
Burn white-hot, stove.
Spill the pearls, small and big,
Neither on satin, nor on velvet,
But on a silver plate.
Cry, Akulina,
Before your dear father. . . .

Then the bride brings her best nuptial bedding and lays it down on the floor for her girlfriends to spend the night. She herself lies down on the edge of this bed, closest to the door. In the morning she is the first to awake, and she rouses the rest with a song:

Get up, my dear friends,
Get up and wash yourselves with spring water,
Dry yourselves with a white towel.
The white dawn is rising,
My adversaries are getting up,
They get up and are about
To tear me away from my father and mother,
And from my dear girlfriends.

The girls get up and go to the groom's house for breakfast. Afterwards, they return and have breakfast with the bride. All the while they honor the bride and the groom with songs and receive small payments for their singing.

Each village has its own specialists to participate in the wedding ceremony, and most important are the female song leaders. Almost every village has one woman who knows the wedding songs better than anyone else. She is invited to weddings as the song leader. The other singers are girlfriends of the bride and relatives of the couple, and for their performance they collect money that is later divided equally among them. The payment, however, is very small, and the singers come mostly for refreshments and vodka.

[Once the breakfasts are completed,] the bride's girlfriends begin preparing her for the wedding ceremony. They undo her braid and comb out the hair,[2] while she laments:

> My dear girlfriends,
> Do not unweave my auburn tresses,
> Do not remove the scarlet ribbon,
> Spare my maidenly beauty;
> Do not don me with wifely drabness,
> Maidenly beauty is fleeting,
> The dreariness of womanhood is endless.

Then the bride is dressed in a blouse, skirts, a sarafan, shoes, and so forth.

In some villages, women wear sarafans to the wedding ceremony, and only afterwards put on the checkered or striped woolen skirt known as a *panyova* that identifies an engaged or married woman. In other villages, a woman wears a *panyova* during the wedding ceremony. She puts it on in the following manner: She stands on a bench in her shift while her brother holds the *panyova* so that she can jump into it. For a long time she resists, turning away and saying: "I'll jump if I want to, and I won't if I don't." Her mother prevails upon her with words like these: "Jump in, my child. Jump in, my dear. You can't remain a maiden for the rest of your life. Be smart, be sensible." Finally the young woman jumps into the *panyova,* and her brother ties it.

The groom arrives with his entourage. The bride's father seats her at the table. If the bride's father has died, she is assisted by her godfather and intones the lament: "A day is bleak without the sun, as my party is bleak without my dear father."

The groom steps down from the cart. At this moment he is accosted by the female members of the bride's family. They wear fur coats inside out and make frightening gestures with stakes and

2. The wearing of a single braid was the sign of an unmarried woman, and this act of uncombing it had powerful symbolic significance in marking the bride's move from her natal family to her husband's. In connection with the marriage ceremony, the newly wedded woman's hair was woven into two braids.

oven forks, intended to prevent the "intruder" from entering the house. Finally, the best man gives the women vodka, and they let the groom pass. When the groom enters the house, the bride is seated at the table surrounded by her father, godfather, and brothers, all brandishing whips and cudgels. They block the groom's path so that he cannot take a seat next to his bride at the table. The groom and his entourage, also with whips in their hands, approach the table and demand to receive the bride. Now the "selling of the bride" begins. Her father places a five-kopeck piece on each corner of the table and says: "Cover these." The best man, acting on the groom's behalf, covers each coin with another. The bride's father then says: "Now gild the bride." The best man places a few more coins in the center of the table. Then the groom is allowed to approach the bride and sit next to her. The bride's mother[3] gathers up the money from the table and gives it to the bride; the mother then serves a small meal, consisting of no more than three dishes. After everyone has eaten and drunk, a candle is lit in front of the icon, and the bride's parents bestow their blessing upon the groom and bride. At the same time, the best man, who is outdoors, walks three times around the groom's cart, holding a cup filled with water and hops, and sprinkles the horses and the people. Bowing to the people, he says: "Orthodox Christian folk! Fair girls are sisters to us, young lads are brothers to us, young women are aunts to us, young men are uncles to us, old men are grandfathers to us, old women are grandmothers to us! Bless our young prince on his way to the temple of God, to face God's judgment, to put on a golden crown, to kiss a golden cross." The people reply: "God bless you. We wish you luck." The best man spills some oats onto the groom's seat in the cart and proceeds to do the same in the bride's cart.[4] The couple emerges from the

3. The choice of "mother" here is arbitrary. Semyonova uses the term *svakha*, the female form of the word for matchmaker. According to the pioneer Russian folklorist Vladimir Dal', the male and female variants of this word can designate the parents of the marriage couple, the godparents, uncles and aunts, or any member of the extended family.

4. As explained later, the grains sprinkled into the carts have the symbolic significance of wishing good fortune and plenty.

This well-dressed peasant woman is wearing a checkered *panyova* skirt beneath her broad apron. Village of Gorodnoe, Spassk district of Riazan province. Courtesy of the Riazan Museum.

house. The groom helps his bride into her cart. The bride, whose face is covered with a towel, is joined in the cart by her godmother, sisters, and aunts. The groom and his company lead the way in his cart.

On the way to the church, as the wedding procession passes through small villages, it is repeatedly halted by the people there, who allow it to continue on its way only after the groom's entourage has passed around drinks. The groom and his party arrive at the church completely drunk, and if any vodka should happen to remain, they will usually take advantage of the commotion to finish it off inside the church. During the ceremony the bride has her hair undone, a sign of sadness. (Unmarried women always appear with their hair down at funerals for their relatives.) After the wedding ceremony, in the church vestibule and with many people looking on, the godmother does up the new wife's hair into two braids, placing an underkerchief (*povoinik*) and a regular kerchief on her head. Then both processions, in the same manner in which they arrived, go to the groom's house, where the parents of the newlyweds are waiting for them. At the doorstep, oats and hops are thrown at the couple. The newlyweds kiss the icon that the husband's mother is holding, and accept bread-and-salt from his father.[5] At this point the young couple break the bread in half and place it on a shelf, a ceremony that is apparently symbolic of the equal property rights of the spouses. The couple take their seats at the table, on which they find two bottles of vodka bound together with a ribbon. The husband's parents untie the ribbon and offer drinks to the guests. The husband's mother removes the kerchief from her daughter-in-law's head and presents her with a new one.

After this, the best man and the godmother take the bridal couple by the hand and lead them to a cabin away from the main house. There the newlyweds will find a chicken pie on the table, and after they have eaten it, the godmother helps the bride to take

5. The presentation of bread and salt was (and remains today) the customary greeting for honored guests in rural Russia.

off her kerchief, sarafan, and shoes, and then proceeds to remove the groom's boots. The groom is expected to have a silver coin in his right boot. The bride will shake the coin out and keep it. Then the best man asks the groom: "Why did you marry?" The groom is supposed to reply: "To provide for a wife and to share a household with her." The godmother directs the same question to the bride, who replies: "To sew shirts for my husband, to clothe him, and to bear him sons." At this point, the best man puts the couple to bed, so that the wife lies on her husband's one arm while he embraces her with the other one. The best man likewise intertwines the legs of the couple and covers them with a blanket before retiring from the cabin with the godmother. Occasionally, before the arrival of the couple, the bride's elder brother and his wife come to the cabin "to warm the bed for the newlyweds." They lie down and embrace in the nuptial bed while the newlyweds eat the chicken pie. When the couple together with the best man approach the bed, the best man exclaims in amazement: "What are this stallion and his mare doing here?" and he tries to drive them out of the bed with a whip. But they refuse and can be persuaded to leave only by an offer of vodka. When the newlyweds are finally alone, many curious eyes and ears (including sometimes children's ears) watch and listen near the door. If the husband learns that his wife is not a virgin, he may mete out punishment at once. The punishment can be quite brutal, including kicking her and pinching her stomach and private parts.

There was a case here of a young man being married against his will because his parents were eager for him to wed a well-to-do young woman whose father was allegedly giving fifteen rubles in dowry. When he found out his wife was not a virgin, he subjected her to such cruel treatment that only a few months after the wedding, this young woman in her prime had turned sickly-looking. "He plucked her underbelly clean," her mother said later. He also would lock her in a shed with only a tiny opening for a window and keep her there for days without food. At night he locked her up and went off to his mistress, a widow who lived in the same village. He habitually dragged his wife by the hair and beat her with whatever was handy. He relented only when the poor woman, whose misfortune it was to be "terribly submissive," became pregnant (despite the beatings and humiliation, he had sexual relations with her), because he could have risked imprisonment for abusing a pregnant woman.

But let me return to the wedding. While the newlyweds stay in the cabin, the party is well under way in the main house. Women and unmarried young people dance dressed as buffoons (*skomorokhi*). After an hour or two, the best man and the godmother go "to get the newlyweds." The godmother takes off the bride's shift and hands it to the godfather. The godfather (or best man) puts the shift on a ceramic plate. The godmother washes the couple, and they get dressed. This time the bride is supposed to wear her brightest sarafan and kerchief (at the wedding ceremony, blue or white colors are usually worn, and they are considered "dull"). When the couple have dressed and are on their way to the house, the best man walks in front of them carrying the plate with the shift on it. In the house he gives the shift to the groom's family for inspection. At the same time the buffoons take dishes off the shelves and break them on the floor as a sign that everything is accomplished.[6] If there are no indications that the bride was unchaste, her parents are offered the first drink with great honors. If it turns out that she was not virtuous, the first drinks are offered to the groom's parents, and the bride's parents are given a mug with a hole in the bottom so that the drink leaks out the moment the best man removes the finger he held over the hole while he was pouring the vodka. If a woman marries a man she was making love to before the wedding, she resorts to the following ruse, with her husband's approval: she hides the shift she was wearing during her last menstrual period and puts it on before the wedding ceremony.

When the godmother wakes up the couple and takes the shift off the young wife, the husband's mother is frequently waiting behind the door to see the garment. I recall an instance when a

6. That is, the hymen is broken.

mother was offended because the shift was taken off her new daughter-in-law in her absence. Another story is recounted about a "loose" girl who, once she was in bed with her new husband, admitted that she was not a virgin and offered him twenty rubles to help her cover up and avoid disgrace. He caught a chick, snapped its head off, and smeared the blood on his wife's shift. Unfortunately, the matchmaker was eavesdropping, and when she handed the girl's shift to the mother-in-law, she explained that they should not bother to display it in the village. "Nowadays this custom is being abandoned because almost all the girls are regarded as unchaste."[7]

The party in the main house goes on until the wee hours. Then the newlyweds retire for the night.

In the morning, the best man and the godmother wake up the bridal couple. The godmother orders the young wife to sweep the floors. Copper coins have been tossed around on the floor beforehand, and the wife is told to give her mother-in-law any coins she finds. This is done to find out if the young wife is a thief, and also to see how well she sweeps the floor. After breakfast the newlyweds have to fetch a tub of water. When they are returning with the water, the father of the groom[8] waylays them and pours the first tub of water on them. Then the neighbors, too, are entitled to douse them with the second and the third tubs. After this, the young wife presents the groom's father a kerchief with which he covers the tub (or pail). From this moment no one can touch the tub, and anyone who does so is whipped by the father. The couple place the tub they have brought at the entrance to the house. At the same time, married women, straddling broomsticks and with their hands covered with chimney soot, chase the neighbors and smear their faces. When the father says "Enough!" the women

7. This final remark, in quotes, like many others in the text, is inserted as an indication of what people in the village generally are saying and does not necessarily belong to the matchmaker.
8. Again, the word is matchmaker (*svat*) and could refer in this context logically to either the father of the groom or the father of the bride. I have chosen to use the former.

stop, and the neighbors come to the tub to wash off the soot. As they do so, they drop a kopeck or two, and occasionally even three kopecks, into the tub, while the young wife is standing nearby with a towel ready to help them dry themselves. "If the women are funny and can make people laugh, the young wife may get as much as a whole ruble."

The wife's parents usually celebrate all night long at the house of their new son-in-law. In the morning the entire family of the groom accompanies the new wife's parents back to their home. Occasionally, the newlyweds also go along. In some villages, processions of this type do not occur, and the whole party just rides off in wagons. A supply of vodka is taken along, and naturally everyone gets drunk. During the ride, they sing songs and bang on scythes, and the women from the groom's family wave at everyone while flourishing the bride's shift over their heads. Of course, this procession is a major attraction for the villagers, who come to gawk at the couple and to make jokes that are quite obscene. The revelers call on relatives in neighboring villages, jump out of the wagons, and dance, all the while showing off the shift.

"Did you ride like this, too? Did they also take your shift for all to see?"

"Of course I did. I couldn't help it. But I shut my eyes and did not look."

[A number of legends and magical beliefs about marriage persisted in the villages studied by Semyonova, and she mentions a few of these.]

There is a legend about a young woman who ordered her brothers to slay her betrothed, and then she arranged a feast at which she regaled the guests with pies baked with his flesh and wine distilled from his brain.

A woman who seeks to charm a man into making love to her washes the menstrual blood off her shift and secretly places the blood—or, more accurately, water with traces of the blood in it—in the kvass or tea that she offers to the object of her desire.

Lovers pledge fidelity by making an oath on the Holy Sacraments. They say, for example: "May I forever be denied the Sacraments if I fail to marry you." They may also pledge their troth to one another by a vow to "Moist Mother Earth," and occasionally they eat some soil to affirm the oath. But the strongest and most inviolable oath is one made on the Holy Sacraments.

At the wedding ceremony, the following superstitions are common:

1. When the groom arrives to take the bride to the church and pays his way, as they say, through the entryway to the main room of the house, he must be preceded into the room by a blood relative of the bride, lest as [an unaccompanied] "stranger" he bring trouble and discord to the bride's family.

2. The best man watches the behavior of the horses before the departure of the couple. If the horses are standing with their heads down, it means the couple will live unhappily. If the horses are in good spirits but quiet, the couple will live in peace. If the horses are violent, the newlyweds will live in discord.

3. The bride and the groom are seated on oats. This is supposed to bring wealth into the family.

4. If the husband begins to undo his wife's hair himself after the wedding ceremony, this too will ensure accord in family life.

5. Returning from the church, the young wife, on entering the house, grabs the lintel with both hands so that "the husband will love her."

6. When the mother-in-law shows the couple to the table, no one should pass between the husband and wife. Otherwise they will live in discord.

7. Sorcerers and witches are feared at the time of the wedding, for it is easiest to put a curse on the couple when they are in the church or returning home after the ceremony. In the church a spell can be cast "through the wind" onto the couple's backs. When newlyweds enter the house, it is not difficult to toss in their path a piece of string tied into a knot with a spell on it. The effects of such

a curse may be lack of affection between the husband and wife, illness, lack of appetite, and the like.[9]

In former times, the father of an "unchaste" bride had to wear a yoke on the morning following the wedding after the discovery of his daughter's shame. The former partner of an "unchaste" woman may spread a bast mat on the church's porch as the newlyweds exit after the ceremony.

[Now we learn about the expenses connected with the village's fall festival, during which weddings were usually held.][10]

The harvest was good, and this year the village's big annual holiday surrounding St. Michael's Day was celebrated for an entire week. The expenditures for it varied according to the wealth of particular households. The well-to-do peasant Ivan Lunkov, whose family consists of seventeen members and produces a yearly turnover of 500 rubles, purchased two and a half pails of vodka [the equivalent of 8.12 gallons or fifty bottles] at 5.5 rubles per pail; he slaughtered eight sheep (a sheep costs 3–3.5 rubles), one hog at 4 rubles, and provided various other foods, including flour, groats, cabbage, cucumbers, pickled apples, sunflower seeds, nuts, bagels, tea, and sugar, in all amounting to 8–10 rubles. So, the total outlay for his holiday could not have been less than 50 rubles.

Vasilii Yeryomin, a peasant of average means (a yearly turnover of 80–100 rubles), spent about 18 rubles on the holiday festivities. He slaughtered an ox worth 10 rubles, bought a half-pail of vodka [ten bottles] for 3.2 rubles, and so forth.

The poor peasant Ustin Guskov had to lay out 9 rubles to entertain his relatives. He purchased a "pitiable" one and a half pounds [of meat apparently] for 4.5 rubles, one quarter-pail [five bottles] of vodka for 1.6 rubles, and used up 108 pounds of flour on pirogs, plus some butter and millet.

9. Here are expressed the dangers associated with liminality. When people are in transition from one stable category of being to another, they are most vulnerable to the action of evil spirits and must be especially alert to defend themselves from these forces.

10. The following three paragraphs are from AGO, f. 109, d. 170, ch. 4, l. 1.

[The published version of Semyonova's study contains two more reports on what are evidently actual marriages. These are rendered in conversational form.]

A woman who recently married off her son tells the following story:

"Sinner that I am, I listened to them talking on their first night. They apparently had been having fun and were so quiet that I was going to leave when I heard Ivan say to her: 'I did not even dream you would marry me!' 'Why so?' 'Well, at the engagement party you looked so nice, and I am pockmarked and cross-eyed. I thought you would turn me down.' The girl sighed: 'Well, I didn't. Maybe now you will treat me better for my good heart.' I laughed at this. She is a quiet girl, all right. You don't need any better. To tell the truth, Ivan does not have the looks, although he is my own child. Moreover, at twenty-two he is rather old for her, already past the draft age, while she is just seventeen. But she is an orphan and poverty-stricken. She really owns nothing. Whatever she did have was lost last year when she and her mother were burned out of house and home and escaped with nothing but the shirts on their backs. Since then they have been living with whoever will give them shelter [*po fateram*]. We, thank goodness, eat our own bread! And, indeed, my Vaniushka is a gentle boy and a good provider."

From a conversation between two peasant women:

"Have you heard that the master's horseherd Ilya got married?"

"You don't say!"

"No kidding. And he's found a really nice girl, one from Sergeevka."

"But wasn't he courting Nastasia?"

"So what if he was? She turned him down, saying she wouldn't marry a drunkard. The other day he went to the master to get his last payment and says: 'Congratulate me, I've gotten married!' And he is crying and wiping away the tears with his fist. He loved Nastasia very much, really yearned for her. On his way back from the master's, he met with Nastasia in a barn, and they got into a long conversation. They felt really sorry for one another, and they were both weeping and kissing."

"Good gracious!"

"Just as they say: it is one thing to fool around, and quite another to get married."

7

❖❖❖

INFANTICIDE, EMOTION, SEXUAL DISORDER, DRINK AND FOOD

As its title reveals, this chapter covers a variety of subjects. Not only the chapter itself but subsections of it have been built out of widely scattered pieces of Semyonova's account and notes. The result, though still a hodge-podge, has the virtue of greater coherence than the original text. Nevertheless, I occasionally have had to insert transitional comments to avoid too sharp a turn in the discussion.

Among a new wife's most important tasks was to reproduce a new generation. Not until she had a surviving child was she regarded as a full-fledged member of her new household. Since Semyonova has already dealt with the issue of childbirth and with child rearing, such as it was in Russian peasant life, she writes little about it in her subsequent notes. But here I wanted to include a few comments she makes on the length of confinement for birthing mothers, sexual contacts between husband and wife, illegitimacy, lullabies, and related topics.

Among these, the topic of infanticide returns. Semyonova's observations are disturbing to modern readers, but there is no reason to doubt their accuracy. My own recent researches on this question suggest that in many parts of Russia, children, unwanted because of illegitimacy, physical malformation, or apparent weakness, met their deaths either quickly through infanticide of the kinds described by Semyonova or more slowly by a reduced level of care and feeding.[1] *Her laconic remark on the low rate of illegitimate births compared to the number of sexually active unmarried women may be taken as one of her measures of the "infanticide gap." She notes as well the illegitimate children of married women, a common enough occurrence in Russian villages, from which many of the men were absent for long periods as migrant laborers or soldiers. We need to keep in mind that these women were not moral monsters. They were charged with maintaining a delicate social and demographic balance; their first duty was to ensure the economic and patriarchal control that ultimately protected their healthy children and the family unit as a whole. Their behavior has to be understood within the context of the precarious subsistence economy in which they lived.*[2]

AFTER GETTING MARRIED, Ivan enjoys a period of grace at home. For the first three days a new husband is a "young prince." The family is indulgent with him and considerate, "if not for his sake, then for his wife's," as they say. The newlyweds receive extra servings of food and are allowed to sleep in during the first three days of

1. For some preliminary results, see my article "Infant Care Cultures in the Russian Empire," in *Russia's Women: Accommodation, Resistance, Transformation*, ed. Barbara Clements, Barbara Engel, and Christine Worobec (Berkeley: University of California Press, 1991), 471-89.

2. On the role of the men in distancing themselves from these decisions on life and death, see the introduction to this book. Similar behavior by families in poor Third World countries of the present day has been recorded by sociologists. See, for example, Susan C. M. Scrimshaw, "Infant Mortality and Behavior in the Regulation of Family Size," *Population and Development Review*, 4:3 (September 1978), 383-403; Monica Das Gupta, "Selective Discrimination against Female Children in Rural Punjab, India," *Population and Development Review*, 13:1 (March 1987), 77-100; Nancy Scheper-Hughes, "Culture, Scarcity, and Maternal Thinking: Maternal Detachment and Infant Survival in a Brazilian Shantytown," *Ethos*, 13:4 (Winter 1985), 281-304.

celebration, but after that, they work, like everyone else. The groom is told something like: "You were young, but now you are a veteran, got yourself a wife, so get to work." The bride is treated more leniently, for she is new in the family. She enjoys certain benefits, for instance in food. Thus, pampering consists of fattening up a prospective worker, three days of the easy life, and the privilege of sleeping outside in a barn or storeroom while the weather is warm [affording the newlyweds some privacy].

In the first few days after the wedding, the young wife talks with her husband in an effort to find out whatever she can about each member of his family, and occasionally she expresses her concern for the future. She also discusses the customs in her husband's household. If the young husband likes her, he naturally tries to reassure her and to explain the way things are and how she can best get along with her mother-in-law and father-in-law.

[When a baby is born,] according to tradition, husband and wife should resume sexual relations six weeks after the woman's confinement, a time marked by her churching and ritual purification. But this rule is rarely observed. After delivery of the first baby, a husband might be considerate to his wife, but after the second or third baby, he does not wait the customary six weeks. If he is drunk, he will resume relations after a week. Even if he stays sober, he will ordinarily begin sexual relations after only two or three weeks. In general, Ivan's sexual demands on his wife are closely related to his diet and to intoxication. Having eaten his fill in the fall, and especially after a drink, Ivan is almost insatiable. On the other hand, when he is hungry or engaged in the heavy summer field work, Ivan rarely goes near his wife. The wife, of course, is not asked her wishes. He simply yells, "Aksinia, come over here!" and that is it. She knows from his tone of voice what he is looking for.

Women age fast so far as their looks are concerned. Yet despite unfavorable conditions for their health, despite even diseases and malnutrition, they sometimes bear children at the age of fifty, and babies are very often born to women in their mid-forties. I know of a woman who gave birth when she was sixty-three years old. Her husband was the same age. She died at the age of sixty-seven, but her husband is still alive and has as his "heir" this twelve-year-old son.

There are also many instances of older men who are still full of energy while their wives are failing badly. This situation sometimes results in what is known as *snokhachestvo*, that is, sexual relations between a man and his daughter-in-law (this also happens occasionally in cases of widowers with married sons).[3]

The rate of illegitimate births for unmarried women is, in fact, very low compared with the number of "loose" girls.

In the big village of B (population 1,200), one, two, or even three times a year a scandal breaks out about an illegitimate pregnancy. Babies in these cases are sent to [the imperial foundling home in] Moscow, but killings of the newborn also occur. In the past four years, there have been two notorious cases of infanticide in the village and in its surrounding parish, cases in which the mothers were tried. The sentence in each case was a few months of imprisonment.

In practice, the number of these killings is higher, if the illegitimate infants of soldiers' wives and other married women are taken into account. Frequently the illegitimacy of these babies is known only to the family, and a killing committed within the family is impossible to prove. I have always been suspicious of cases of reported accidental smothering of babies, since it is very easy to roll over on a baby and intentionally smother it while pretending that it happened by accident in sleep.

Not all babies are subject to killing, but illegitimate ones are very likely to be. A weak baby that is a burden to its mother is not killed, although its parents will grumble at its existence and con-

3. For a recent study of the unenviable position of a Russian daughter-in-law, see Beatrice Farnsworth, "The Litigious Daughter-in-Law: Family Relations in Rural Russia in the Second Half of the Nineteenth Century," *Slavic Review*, 45:1 (Spring 1986), 49-64.

stantly express a desire for its death.[4] Among the reasons for infanticide are shame, fear, and finances. An unmarried woman is most likely to kill her baby out of shame. A married woman or a soldier's wife will do so fearing the wrath of her husband or his family, while a widow burdened with children will kill a baby because of economic need (see the accounts [given earlier] of a young married woman who under the pressure of her mother-in-law poisoned her illegitimate baby with matches and of a poor homeless widow who drowned her illegitimate baby in the pond). Older women are very ruthless and cold-blooded about the killing of an illegitimate "whelp," whom they view as a nuisance and a burden. Young women anguish over such a decision and force themselves to kill their babies only when shame or fear causes them to lose their senses, or when they can no longer bear their own and their babies' suffering. Men, from what I could observe, often simply do not know about such killings, even when they occur in their own families, or, if they figure out what is going on, they look the other way. "Damn women are cooking up something, the hell with them, it's no concern of mine" is probably how a man reasons, pushing away any thoughts of what the women are up to.

Leo Tolstoy captured peasant character traits marvelously in a similar situation. Watch the peasants, observe their life closely, and you will see just how accurate Tolstoy's depiction was: the cruelty of old Matryona, the frenzy of Anisia . . . all these are true pictures of peasant life, the way it really is.[5]

4. A Russian folklorist found that about 8 percent of her collection of thousands of lullabies were songs wishing death on babies, presumably weak infants like those mentioned here whose survival was uncertain and who may have been in pain. A. N. Martynova, "Otrazhenie deistvitel'nosti v krest'ianskoi kolybel'noi pesne," *Russkii fol'klor,* 15 (Leningrad, 1975), 145-55.

5. Here Semyonova is referring to a scene in Tolstoy's play *The Power of Darkness,* in which the peasants kill an illegitimate baby and attempt to hide the evidence by burying the corpse in their cellar. L. N. Tolstoi, *Polnoe sobranie sochinenii* (Moscow, 1913), 14:51-52.

The rate of child deaths is highest in the summer during the fast of St. Peter [in June], and especially during the field-work season, when unattended children eat anything they come across: cucumbers, sour apples, and any other vegetation. Diarrhea is the chief cause of child death. As for the death rate, in a majority of homes more than half of all children die. Most women bear from eight to ten or twelve children, of which only three or four survive.[6] [The death of an infant in a poor family that could not support another child was evidently regarded as a blessing, as Semyonova recorded in one of her unpublished field notes.] When a poor family's child dies, people say: "Thank goodness, the Lord thought better of it!"[7]

[The peasant cradle and the lullabies that accompany its rocking played a central role in family life. The cradle was usually made of wood (or a wooden frame with a canvas bottom) and suspended from a small spring attached to a rafter. A rope or thong with a loop fell from the cradle to the floor, enabling the cradle to be rocked by anyone available to sit near it; and Russian cradles were in motion much of the day, by all accounts.]

A woman slips the loop around her foot to rock the baby, while her hands are occupied with some needlework. When the adult women force a small girl to rock the cradle, she may rock it so hard that the baby flies out. "Mashka, take it easy, you fool, make sure you don't flip the child onto the floor!" is the usual rebuke to the child.

Lullabies commonly sung today:

> Hush, hush, hushaby my baby,
> Don't lie near the edge of the bed.
> The gray wolf will come
> And carry you off to the woods.

6. For the average rates of child survival in late imperial Russia and the causes of infant death, see my "Infant Care Cultures in the Russian Empire," in *Russia's Women: Accommodation, Resistance, Transformation,* cited earlier.

7. Literally, "The Lord took another look" (oglianul'sia Gospod). Arkhiv AN SSSR, f. 609, op.1, d. 26, l. 335.

Or:

> Hush, hush, hushaby my baby,
> I'll give you spankings,
> Twenty-five of them,
> To make you sleep better and deeper.

Or:

> Hush, hush, hushaby my baby.
> A man lives at the end of the village.
> He's neither poor, nor rich,
> He has many children,
> They sit on a bench
> And eat straw.
> I'll make you suffer even more.
> I won't give you anything to eat.
> I won't make a bed for you.

Or:

> Hush, hush, hushaby my baby.
> Sleep, sleep, fall asleep
> Let peace overtake you.

The last-quoted lullaby is the most common. The women say: "I have no time to think up rhymes; I've got enough worries as it is. All you can say is the ordinary 'Sleep, sleep, may peace overtake you.' . . . It is only when there is not much to do and you start thinking about the children, and it upsets you just to look at them, then you might hit on some of the old rhymes, though rarely."

[Semyonova wonders about the quality of personal relations between husband and wife, and in this connection she explores the issues of peasant affect and humor.]

The question of how a peasant husband might show affection for his wife has long interested me. At one time, I believed that peasants simply do not express their emotions, since there are absolutely no external signs of a husband's feelings toward his wife, even in young couples. But the following story recently caused me to reconsider this issue. "Take Petrukha!" say the local women. "Look how he cares for his wife! I wonder if there is another woman as lucky as she in the village!"

Petrukha, an ordinary peasant, is our coachman, but a coachman "on temporary leave from the plow," as it were. I have long known him as a plain, quiet man, while his wife is a shrewd and clever, if selfish, woman. I also know that Petrukha gave up drinking after he got drunk at a wedding and nearly drowned in a pond, and that he does not beat his wife. He is not much of a manager, but his wife is first-rate and "thinks through" everything carefully, such as how to do the sowing, the mowing of hay, the purchasing of a cow, and the like. At his wife's slightest call, Petrukha, who is not capable even of providing for the morrow, rushes to the village to do whatever she asks of him. If his friends prevent him from going during the day, he will sneak out at night. And in case of discovery, he has anticipated the accusation and eagerly provides an explanation: "My missus had an idea to get a head start on binding the millet into sheaves. Well, you could see it was going to rain, so I went out at night and mowed the lot for her." If his wife tells him that the house is not properly caulked for the winter, he will not rest until he finds the time to patch up the place and put her mind at ease. Before he married eight or nine years ago following his military service, Petrukha was the most slovenly fellow in the village. Unfortunately, men like Petrukha and the type of relationship he has with his wife are rare indeed. To tell the truth, this is the only case I know of.

[Then Semyonova tells of a sight that she assumes a German would interpret through a romantic metaphor, whereas the Russian applied a competitive one.]

In the orchard, felling trees.

Looking at two young intertwined trees, a birch and a linden, that grow, as it were, from the same root, I say:

"It is amazing how intertwined they are!"

To which the gardener replies: "They argue which one will win."

The laborer, warming to the subject, adds: "I bet the linden will beat it. Birch is no match for linden."

The Germans would surely have said something about two enamored beings, for it is supposed to be so in an orchard, where the atmosphere is conducive to sentimental thoughts. . . .

[Further anecdotes concern personal expression and humor.]

Yesterday I was in our garden and could unseen watch passers-by on the road leading to the village. This year the harvest was good, and there is more traffic on the road. I saw two young men walking along silently eating sunflower seeds. I approached the gate and asked one of them, Boris, where they were going. My question seemed to startle them out of their "sleep walk." Boris told me that they were on their way to drink tea in Muraevnia. This was said with a completely blank look, with no trace of a smile.

Then a peasant couple passed by in the usual single file, like a gander and his goose, the man leading the way and the woman in his wake. They had been to the mill to sell cabbage. Again, what sullen and dejected looks they wore on their faces! I watched them for a few minutes as they walked by, oblivious of my presence. Only once did the man turn to his wife, and then merely to ask for paper to make a cigarette. The woman pulled out a package she was carrying on her bosom, tore off a scrap of paper, and passed it to her husband. His gnarled fingers rolled a cigarette, and the couple resumed their silent journey.

Only when peasants are drunk or quarreling can their voices be heard from afar. When the men are drunk, they have an obscene comment for every passing woman. A woman might reply: "You'd better go to church, Ivan. I reckon you've never been there." And the man in rebuttal: "Me? Go to a priest? What do I need with a piece of shit like him? He still hasn't gotten around to tying the knot between you and me." This is a relatively good-natured and mild jest. It is a big success with the man's buddies, and they burst out laughing. But the laughter is hard and fitful. They do not sound as if they are really enjoying themselves.

Husbands and wives speak very little with each other. But if a few women get together, the discussion can be animated, at least more so than in a group of men. When women walk together down the street, they are never silent. They ramble on about the minutiae of their domestic life. Their laughter also strikes me as livelier and more cheerful than that of the men.

Of course, sometimes you can hear genuinely hearty laughter from the men. I have noticed, for example, that some of the peasant men never fail to evoke chuckles from their fellow farm workers or fellow villagers. As soon as the broad beard or fat face of such a peasant comes into view, everyone bursts into laughter. Usually the object of this merriment is a person who carries himself with dignity, may be quite handsome, and strikes a fine figure. Yet he is met with shrieks of laughter. It seems that the reason for the merriment lies in the man's pretention; peasants do not like "uppityness" and want to make it look ridiculous. It is the air of self-importance that elicits the laughter, and the angrier the target of the fun becomes, the greater the laughter. Usually, the shabbiest-looking peasants take the most delight in this spectacle. Of course, they themselves are never the target of laughter. The peasants' laughter is prolonged, and they literally shriek with merriment, gasping for air and doubling over as if they wished to hide completely their unassuming faces.

Unfortunately, when the possessor of this "laughable" deportment is a wealthy farmer (kulak), you do not hear any laughter. Peasants laugh at their "buddies," and a kulak is hardly a "buddy."

A dozen female and two male farm workers are preparing to return from the landlord's threshing barn. It is cold, and a snowstorm is blowing. Two of the women linger near a pile of oats heaped at the barn's doorway. Both women, Anisia and Aleksandra, are originally from the same village, but Aleksandra moved after her marriage. Now Anisia is visiting with her sister in the village where Aleksandra also currently lives. Aleksandra has invited her old friend to keep her company at the threshing barn and at the same time to earn good money, thirty kopecks a day. The overseer (*barskii starosta*) stands nearby.

ANISIA (a woman in her thirties): "Aleksandra, dear, look for my shawl, I left it here somewhere in the oats."

ALEKSANDRA (a soldier's wife), rummaging in the pile: "I can't seem to find it."

THE OVERSEER: "Why are you messing around in the oats? Get on home!"

ANISIA: "My shawl must be there . . ."

OVERSEER: "What crap! The thing costs fifteen kopecks. It's not exactly a recent wedding present. You'll make it home without a shawl. . . . Get moving!"

ANISIA (sounding hurt): "Even if it cost only five kopecks, it's still dear to me."

ALEKSANDRA: "Here it is."

The overseer locks the barn, and he and the two stragglers catch up with the other women, who are struggling against the wind.

ANISIA (tying the shawl): "Thank you, dear. . . . (Then after a while) Is your husband coming home soon?"

ALEKSANDRA (sighs): "He's got two more years to serve."

OVERSEER (laughs): "She said just the other day she'd be happy if he had another year to go."

ALEKSANDRA: "You're lying. I've cried my head off, just look at me. How can you say such a thing—that I'd be 'happy'?"

OVERSEER (still laughing): "Hey, Anisia, the other day they told [Aleksandra] that her husband, Pavel, was killed in China, and she started to dance."

ALEKSANDRA: "Go to hell, damn you!"

OVERSEER: "Mikolka, why are you hanging around the girls? You haven't fed the animals yet."

ALYOSHKA: "Look, there he is, hiding behind Mashka, warming up."

The women laugh. The wind throws a cloud of tiny sharp snowflakes in their faces.

ANISIA: "It's freezing! I can't wait to get back to the house and lie down on the stove."

MASHKA (a fat, ruddy woman): "Lying on the stove gets boring."

Men and women working in front of barns for the storage of grain. Village of Sergeevo, Riazan district of Riazan province. Courtesy of the Riazan Museum.

ALEKSANDRA: "Maybe it's boring. But it's better than out here. You warm up first on one side, then on the other." (She starts singing.)

OVERSEER: "Hey, smarty, why start hollering? Not cold enough for you?"

ALEKSANDRA: "One song is all I know."

The women giggle.

ALEKSANDRA: "If I had wings, I would fly to him."

The women giggle again. One of them says: "Sure, and he'd give you a beating."

Aleksandra (addressing Anisia): "No, he wrote me[8] a letter the other day, says, 'If I had eight wings, I would fly to you every day.' That's what he says."

Here is the letter from Aleksandra's husband, Pavel:

"A letter home. From your son. My first duty is to make haste to inform you that at present I am safe and sound. I bow humbly to my dear mother Marfa Vasilevna, and may God grant you good health and a speedy and successful conclusion to all your endeavors. I also pray that peace and goodness may exist in both the military and civil service so long as I live. I also give best regards to my dear brother Demian Ivanovich and pray the Lord grant you good health and the best of everything. I also give my best regards to my dear spouse, Aleksandra Artemovna; I kiss you countless times on your sweet lips as if I were with you and send you my deepest husbandly respects, and may God grant you good health, a speedy and successful conclusion to all your endeavors, and a happy heart. I also give my best greetings to my dear and fondly remembered children, Vladimir Pavlovich and Avdotia Pavlovna. I send you my parental blessing; may peace accompany you all your days. Dear mother, forgive me for not writing you for a long time. I did not know that you had sent me money, which reached me only recently. I thank you from the bottom of my heart for this dear present. You think, dear mother, that I am cross with you, but I am not, the opposite is true—I miss you very much. If I had four big wings, I would fly to you and to my dear wife every day. I also give my best regards to my godparents, first to my godfather, Artem Kuzmich, and his wife, Avdotia Ilinishna, and to their children, and may God grant them all good health and the best of everything. I also give regards to my godmother and her spouse, Ilia Andreevich; may God grant them good health and a speedy and successful conclusion to all their endeavors. I also give my greetings to my aunt Anisia Stepanovna and my brother Pyotr

8. The letter, as we learn below, is really written to his entire family.

Nikolaevich, along with his spouse and children; may God grant them good health and the best of everything. I also give regards to Yegor Terentievich and his spouse, Liubov Nikolaevna, and their children, and may God grant them good health and the best of everything. Give my regards also to all our other relatives and friends. May the Lord grant them good health and Godspeed in all their endeavors. With this, I bid you farewell. I am safe and sound here, thank God. Pavel Ivanov Openkin."

[The family associated with this letter seemed to be managing without the son who was in the army. But the loss of a critical family member to the military or to death could bring a crisis in a household's economy. This, in turn, led to the need to beg, and some of the beggars, as Semyonova points out, especially outsiders to the village such as Gypsies and blind men, could be a source of sexual disorder. In this connection, she records a humorous story about the blind men.]

Beggars are usually old people and children, and to a lesser extent young and middle-aged women. Children begin begging as early as the age of six. Children and other members of a peasant family resort to begging when there is not enough food in the house and no means to procure it. When a family has to send one of its own to beg for the first time, it usually does so with tears and lamentations.

There are also permanent beggars. These include single, homeless old men and women, cripples, blind people, imbeciles, and village fools. Sometimes these wretches are not from the poorest families, but being unable to work, they are sent to beg so as to be of some use to their households. Homeless beggars, both men and women, usually find a poor family and in return for lodgings share with the family some of their daily take. I knew one "simpleton," about forty years of age, a huge man of nearly seven feet, who because of his condition was doing quite well in soliciting donations. He lived in a poor family composed of a father, mother, and two children. This "holy fool," who was nicknamed Kupolai,[9] was having an intimate relationship with the woman of the house. The family treasured him as a source of income, yet when he died, they did not bother to bury him and instead sought out a distant relative of his in another village to do the job.

According to stories told by the peasants, the real Don Juans among the beggars are the blind men, who make their rounds with boys as their seeing-eye guides. The blind men sing religious verses and stay for the night wherever they find hospitality. So some of our "Ivans" are the product of such liaisons; one might be the child of a blind man, another of a Gypsy, or yet another of a holy fool or of a drunkard pretending to be a holy fool. Not long ago, no more than five years back, Gypsies would make camp for the winter in the villages and move in with peasant families. This practice has since been forbidden. Peasant women really go for Gypsy men.

Boccaccio à la russe

"Those blind fellows are real stallions. Wild, that's what they are! It is simply indescribable how they beat the boys they employ as seeing-eye guides. A woman can't pass by, but they order the boys to grab hold of her.

"There was this one blind man who beat his guide boy so hard that the boy decided to bring him a mare instead of a woman. When the blind fellow mounted the mare from behind, it kicked him right in the face and sent him flying. And what did he say? 'She's real hot, I've never seen a woman so wild in my life!'"

[Excessive consumption of hard liquor might also be seen as a form of disorder, but it was so integral a part of Russian peasant

9. A "holy fool" (*iurodivyi*) is a person thought to be endowed by God with the power to foretell the future. The nickname given to this holy fool means "cupola" and refers to his height, as high as a church cupola. Peasants often referred to one another, and not just to eccentric persons, by nicknames that were associated with their physical appearance.

life, as we have already seen, that it can also be understood as belonging to the normal rhythm of daily life.]

Drinking is a temptation no one can withstand. Prodigious amounts of alcohol are consumed at wedding parties. I myself have attended weddings at which nine-and ten-year-old girls were made to drink so that they would dance for everyone's entertainment. Reportedly they make the boys drink "for fun," too. Most youngsters start drinking on a dare.

There are some occasions at which drunkenness is required by tradition. For example, young men are expected to drink before they are drafted. Men who are scheduled to appear at the drafting station in late fall are called "able-bodied" (*godnye*). In the period following the field-work season and up to the time of their conscription, the "able-bodied" young men are supposed to enjoy themselves. When their own money runs short, their families supply them with funds to continue their merriment. All the "able-bodied" men of a village go around together having their good time. Anyone who does not keep up with the others is considered "dishonored," and to avoid this, a young man will sacrifice even his and his family's last kopeck. The revelry takes place both in the tavern and in the streets, and is accompanied by much rowdiness. All the "able-bodied" men are supposed to carry accordions, which they play all night long, right up to sunrise. With this accompaniment to their drunken singing, the whole crowd stalks around the village, smashing window panes and indulging in most unseemly pranks. These capers are regarded with tolerance. "What's the uproar going on outside?" someone will ask. "Oh, it's just the 'able-bodied' men making merry . . . ," and the term "able-bodied men" both explains and justifies everything. Frequently the "able-bodied" engage in a game of pitch and toss, although this activity is banned by the authorities.

The best occasion for young people to get drunk for the first time is the annual festival, which in this region takes place in connection with St. Michael's Day. On that holiday, every person in the parish is drunk. In a good year the festival lasts for a week, but even when the crops are poor, people manage to go on a spree for three days. There is also a great deal of drinking at Shrovetide. This is the time for traveling to visit relatives, and for riding troikas. Accidents abound in the springtime [as a result of drunkenness]. Some people drown in water-filled ravines. Others are crushed under falling wagons; a drunken peasant will have a wagon tip over on him, and that is the end of him. Considerably less drinking occurs on Christmas and Easter.

At a fair I witnessed a woman (a widow) walking with her drunken boyfriend, a farm laborer, who, predictably, was squeezing out a tune on his accordion. The woman, too, was drunk and heading back to the tavern for a drink. When her thirteen-year-old daughter accosted her and reproached her for spending their money on alcohol and degrading herself, the woman's companion reacted violently and beat the girl so mercilessly that it was pitiful to watch. And none of the men lifted a finger to stop him. The women alone reacted by howling.

A young man may be introduced to heavy drinking during the street parties. Street parties provide a brisk trade for the bootleg establishment that is invariably operated in every village, usually by some widow. The drinks are served in a shkalik, a medium-sized glass containing approximately two ounces. A moderate drinker will order two or three shkaliks in a row. Peasants claim they drink "to drown their sorrows" or "to ease their troubled minds." Frequently vodka becomes indispensable for them. At meetings of the village council, it is customary to take turns paying for drinks. When visiting someone's house, a peasant will be pleased with the refreshments only if a fair amount of alcohol is served. Snacks are of much less concern. Peasants are naturally more willing to drink while on a visit or in a tavern than at home. When there is a bootleg establishment in the village, men are not likely to drink at all at home, except at family occasions, such as weddings and baptismal dinners.

Drinking also accompanies delivery of the first load of grain for grinding. The miller provides the liquor, for which he is repaid with grain. Another occasion for general drunkenness is seasonal field work for the landlord (usually mowing and transportation of produce to town), who by way of payment treats the peasants to refreshments. On these occasions dreadful fights break out and can result in maiming or even killing with a scythe. When the oats are taken to town for sale, the occasion is celebrated with drinking. Needless to say, service in the army is also a school for drinking. When a group of young horseherds includes a few older boys, say about age sixteen or seventeen, they instruct the younger ones to steal liquor from home when their parents are away. The loot is then shared by all, not infrequently including boys ten to twelve years old.

[This discussion of drink leads naturally to a consideration of peasant diet and drinking in connection with it.]

During the field-work season, a peasant gets up very early. After bowing before the icon and praying "My Lord Jesus Christ, in the name of the Father, the Son, and the Holy Ghost. Amen," he sets out to work. But sometimes he leaves right away for work and just makes the sign of the cross along the way. Prayers are also said before the night rest, which lasts two or three hours. Peasants begin mowing on an empty stomach, before breakfast when the sun is not up yet. Occasionally the grain is harvested at night under the full moon, when the dew and the cold keep the ears from shedding their seeds. At seven or eight in the morning, peasants return home and have their breakfast, consisting of potatoes and bread. During the work season, peasants are happy for the chance to drink one or two shkaliks of vodka for refreshment at breakfast, dinner, and supper. If there is a tavern in the village, peasants drop in there after breakfast and have their shkalik before they return to the field, where they work until the noon dinner break.

Dinner consists of cabbage soup, porridge (kasha), or, again, potatoes and bread. The soup, of course, has no meat in it, just cabbage, but occasionally sour cream is added. Potatoes are mixed with kvass and onions. The porridge—usually millet—is eaten either with milk, in what is known as the thin form (*kulesh*), or in a thicker form made with hemp-seed oil. After dinner, the peasants take a rest and then return to the fields. They take along

A father plows while his son looks on. Plowing was work normally left to men. Courtesy of the Library of Congress.

some bread for an afternoon snack sometime between three and five o'clock. When the sun sets, the peasants go home, and at about nine in the evening they eat their supper, which is warmed-over dinner, with the possible addition of skim milk.

On Sundays and holidays peasants stay in bed till late and get up only before mass. (An exception is made, however, when it is hot at harvest time and the crops need to be cut promptly before they dry out. At these times, peasants work on Sundays as well.) Peasants attend mass at the nearest village with a church (*selo*). On the way they may find time to visit a tavern and down a shkalik or two. I do not believe that in church the peasants are occupied with thoughts about the mass and God: they are burdened with too many other worries, especially during the field-work season. Peasants are a bit intimidated by the priest, who is much given to sermonizing about and denouncing his parishioners' indolence and lack of concern for God's temple, sometimes while pointing at negligent parishioners and reminding them of their various sins. After the service, abstemious peasants go home, while others head for the tavern, where everyone gets drunk. The more sober peasants eat dinner at home, rest, and then "just sit" till the evening, talking about their affairs and discussing the harvest and related subjects. Yet even back in the home village, there are opportunities to have a drink, and it is unlikely that a peasant will let a Sunday go by without having one. In the evening, women get a feeling for the amount of alcohol consumed by their husbands by the intensity of the beatings they receive. Then everything is quiet. The next morning a heavy head reminds them of the day before.

In winter peasants get up at six A.M. and feed the livestock. The rest of the time passes mostly in slumber, unless there is some threshing or weaving of bast shoes to do.

Foods that can be found on a peasant's table only during the annual festival, or during a wedding or baptismal dinner, include pancakes (*bliny*), meat (veal designated for holidays—*uboina*), potato fritters (*drachena*), buns (*pyshki*), *salamata* (a kind of thin gruel), *kalinnik* (a kind of cake), fritters (*olad'i*), and cabbage soup with corned beef (*solonina*).

During a famine, peasant meals consist of stale bread moistened in water and mixed with goosefoot. The men make extra efforts to find any type of work, and sometimes the entire family goes out to beg. As soon as the snow melts, hungry children pick roots and herbs to eat, such as sorrel and clover. Peasants also make soup with goutweed (*Aegopodium podagraria*).

[Sickness was a frequent visitor in peasant homes, and for the most part peasants treated themselves with home remedies or sought the help of a village healer, who would employ incantations, physical manipulation, or herbal cures. Semyonova in her few notes about disease emphasizes the links between illness, diet, and work.]

Fever is very common in our parts. Among the non-epidemic and non-contagious diseases, most common is indigestion resulting from excessive drinking or from returning to meat and milk products at the end of a fast. Peasants contract a very acute strain of this illness that is accompanied by a stomachache and a pain in the pit of the stomach, with colic and vomiting. A peasant who is suffering these severe symptoms tends to think that he is going to die and sends for a priest. In the work season, peasants often catch colds and lose their voices ("My whole chest is blocked up," they report) because they drink cold water when they are overheated.[10] Flushed with heat and "assaulted by thirst," as the peasants say, they cannot seem to get enough to drink and will take water from any source available. They drink from a roadside ditch, from a muddy puddle, from a swamp, wherever they can find some water to quench their thirst. Tapeworms and roundworms are common among peasants. In the fall, the water in the river is literally poisoned by hemp that is soaked there until the first frosts. There are cases of poisoning with this water. In the fall, women frequently catch chills when bathing sheep in the cold water prior to shearing.

[As for grooming and washing,][11] married women comb their hair once every six weeks. Some of them may do it every three weeks. Teenage girls sometimes comb their hair every day, but in any case once a week. They wash their hands once a day without soap. They wash in the morning and dry themselves off with their sleeves, the hems of their skirts, or their aprons. Unmarried women wash with soap morning, noon, and evening. Sometimes mothers wash their children with water that they first put in their mouths to warm up. They do not rinse out their mouths [after eating]. Every Saturday they crawl into the stove [for a kind of sauna], and occasionally they bathe in the barn with hot water.

10. Even today Russians seem to think that drinking cold water when one is overheated will cause colds and other illnesses. The cause of illness is no doubt the unclean sources of the cold water, as suggested two sentences below, but the association in the minds of the people was (and is) with the temperature of the water.

11. The following passage is from Semyonova's unpublished field notes in Arkhiv AN SSSR, f. 906, op. 1, d. 26, l. 332.

8

❖❖❖

HOUSING, PROPERTY, TRADES, BUDGETS, AND RELIGIOUS BELIEF

*This chapter begins with a description of peasant living quarters, but Semyonova quickly gets caught up in telling about the stifling atmosphere of houses heated by "black stoves." (Such chimneyless homes, called in Russian "smokey houses" [*kurnye izby*], were quite common in central and especially northern Russia until the end of the nineteenth century.) Note that the principal fuel in this instance was straw, because Semyonova's village was in the lightly forested Black Earth region. Here the roofs were often thatched, and chimneyless stoves may have been a necessity because burning straw could drift up the flue and land on the thatched roof.*

In the discussion of fire protection that follows, Semyonova tells of the willow trees that furnished a protective barrier against the raging fires that all too regularly consumed Russian villages and towns. The willows had dual and discrepant uses: when alive and green, they formed a screen against flying embers, and (as we read in the court cases cited by Semyonova in chapter 10) when cut and dried out, they served as ignitable fuel.

The next section treats the division of tasks and goods between husband and wife. No formal study of the Russian peasantry can provide a precise division of such things, for each village had its own customs. We can nevertheless see from Semyonova's description of her village that Russian women, even if ideology placed them in a strictly subordinate position, controlled assets of their own and were by no means simply slaves to their husbands.

The information in this chapter about the lending of cows between rich and poor peasants and stories in the next chapter about well-off peasants (kulaks) giving interest-free loans suggest that the crude opposition often seen in peasant studies between exploitative kulaks and their poor exploited neighbors is overdrawn. Households of unequal wealth were able to work out arrangements that provided mutual benefits. Conversely, Semyonova reports cases of naked coercion used against persons who refused to support the local political boss or who could not pay their taxes on time, situations that were taken advantage of by some wealthy peasants. The stories in the next chapter, however, make clear that poor peasants also had ways of getting back at better-off neighbors for whom they had no sympathy. In other words, no simple model can capture the complex lines of solidarity and hostility that marked the relations among village households.

With regard to the peasants' unwillingness to engage in more drudgery than it took to meet the needs of their household, which Semyonova mentions here and elsewhere, students may want to look into the ideas of the Russian economist A. V. Chayanov, who constructed an elaborate and influential theory of peasant economy based on the idea that peasant behavior was different from that assumed by classical economists.[1]

When Semyonova turns to the division of family property at the time of the separation of some members, her discussion can be better understood if one recalls that the large Russian peasant family was composed of a mother and father and their grown sons, together with the wives and children of the sons. Two, three, or more nuclear families might reside in a single household, and personal conflict or lack of space could

1. A. V. Chayanov, *The Theory of Peasant Economy* (Madison: University of Wisconsin Press, 1986).

and did regularly require the separation of one or more of the nuclear units.

The budget included in this chapter is not that of the kind of joint family just described but of a three-generational stem family (in which the oldest generation has been truncated by the death of the husband). The expenses for this family slightly outrun its income, but as the children grow older and begin to contribute to household production, the balance sheet is likely to move into the black. Note, too, that the budget includes payments to the priest and the church. Although her editors did not include any more about this in the published account, I found in Semyonova's archive a breakdown of payments and other demands for money and goods that the priest made of his parishioners, and I have included this material in the chapter. It is clear from her comments about these payments and from her published notes that follow in which she compares the priest to the local folk healers that Semyonova shared the Russian intelligentsia's contempt for the Russian clergy.

Finally, Semyonova speaks of the peasants' belief in higher powers, and she compares their ideas of the tsar and of God. She concludes that their most deeply held beliefs in supernatural power continue to be those associated with the religious and magical notions of pre-Christian Russia.

❖

HOUSES HAVE equal sides that measure from fourteen to twenty-one feet. There are two windows. The entryway (*sentsa*) is usually built with thin, low-quality logs. Just opposite the door from the main room into the entryway is another door leading into the yard. If an entryway is wide enough, it is used for storing horse collars and women's trunks. To the left of the door leading into the house is a bench known as a *konnik* (also *ikonnik* or *okonnik*). Another bench runs along the adjoining wall, the one with the windows in it, and is the longest bench in the house (*peredniaia lavka*). In the corner where these two benches meet, the icons are placed on a shelf. One more bench stands along the wall opposite the entrance and is called a *sudnik*. In the far right-hand corner there is a whitewashed brick stove with a sleeping shelf (*lezhanka*) running along its top. Stoves with chimneys are called "white," while chimneyless stoves are referred to as "black." When a "black" stove is being lighted, the door from the main room into the entryway is left open so that the smoke up to the level of the door is drawn out, but above that level it forms a blue and white blanket through which nothing can be seen. The top of the door is no higher than a rather short person, so that one has to stoop to enter the house (the ceiling itself is only 5′10″ high). A good-sized man finds it difficult to stand up when the stove is being fired, because his eyes will be in the caustic cloud of smoke. Even when seated on a bench, one feels the acrid smoke in the eyes. I myself cannot stay more than ten minutes inside a house while the stove is being fired, but peasants get used to it. Some old people do not even climb down from the top of the stove when it is being lighted; they lie there right in the thick smoke—but they probably have their eyes closed. When the fuel has burned up, the stove door is closed and, as the peasants avow, "it's warm as toast in here." Peasants believe "black" stoves are much warmer than the "white" ones. I do not know if this is true, but I can say that the smoke continues to irritate one's eyes long after the stove door has been shut.

Peasants use straw for fuel. Rye straw is the best for this purpose; the straw of oats and millet is of much poorer quality. Peasants bring straw in at night to sleep on, and then in the morning they feed this straw into the stove. The use of fresh straw each day provides reasonably hygienic bedding for the peasants. But this is so only in years of abundant harvest. In a bad year, whatever little straw they have is given to the livestock; sometimes even straw roofs have to be pulled down to save the animals from starvation. The shortage of straw forces peasants to use their clothes for bedding and to heat the house with dried manure or weeds such as burdock, thistle, and nettles. Accordingly, illnesses increase in such a year. The lack of fresh bedding is one cause. The poor fuel likewise does much damage to the eyes. In the drought years of 1891–1892, around ten people in two of our small villages (each containing about fifteen households) lost their eyesight temporarily or permanently from the smoke of their stoves. The smoke, which was produced by burning dried manure and weeds found on the roadside and in ravines, was so acrid that the victims (mostly old people and children) developed cataracts. All of them were admitted to the regional hospital in town, but three of them never got their eyesight back.[2]

Manure, in addition to being used in lean years as fuel for home heating, is mixed with clay and made into building blocks for clay-walled houses. [For these reasons, among others,] poor peasants fertilize their land very little, spreading no more than twenty cartloads of manure.

Back to the house.

The stretch of the wall from the stove to the wall with the entrance door is also lined with a bench (*zadnik*), which in the corner joins another bench (*pridelok*) that runs up to the entrance door. Next to the protruding corner of the stove there is a post (the same height as the entrance door) that supports a beam, the other end of which rests on the log forming a lintel just above the door. The space between this beam and the wall running parallel to it is covered with planks to form a kind of raised platform or loft, on which older members of the family and small children sleep. The rest of the family is accommodated on the sleeping shelf atop the stove and on the benches lining the walls of the house. In the left-hand corner opposite the entryway stands a table. Normally a peasant's house has one or two short portable benches that are brought to the table for dinner and supper. The floor is made of either hard-packed earth or wooden planks (rough or finished). If

2. For a discussion of the dimensions of this serious and widespread disorder of the eyes in Russian villages, see Nancy M. Frieden, "Child Care: Medical Reform in a Traditionalist Culture," in *The Family in Imperial Russia: New Lines of Historical Research*, ed. David L. Ransel (Urbana: University of Illinois Press, 1978), 236-59.

of planks, these are supported by joists and run across the house parallel to the entrance-door wall. In a floor made of boards, there is usually an opening through which a ladder leads into a pit dug out under the house where potatoes are stored. Above the bench opposite the entrance door, shelves are mounted on the wall to store dishes. Ceiling boards run parallel to the wall with the windows and are supported by a beam that rests on the walls. On the attic side these boards are coated with clay and a layer of dry leaves, and topped off with earth. The roof is supported by rafters and angle brackets. Wattles across the rafters form a base for brushwood, which is then thatched. The lintel is hewn as the walls are being erected, but the door frame and window frames are purchased separately.

In the past, wooden houses were made chiefly of oak, but nowadays willow wood is more often used. Numerous masonry houses are also found, accounting for more than half the homes in a few villages. The clay-walled type of house is becoming increasingly common as we see more and more family divisions and splitting up of property [so that people live in smaller families but with fewer resources]. Many peasants now have neither a threshing barn, a shed, nor even a yard of their own.

Both the masonry and clay-walled houses have the same inside layout as a wooden home. A clay-walled house is built in the following manner: four posts are set to form a square; the spaces between the posts are boarded up with thick planks or logs, and then plastered on both sides with clay. Lastly the house is whitewashed inside and out. The yard, which is also square and measures between twenty-three and fifty-eight feet on a side, is enclosed with a wattle fence and covered with a straw awning. The corners of the yard are boarded up to form pens for livestock. There can be from one to four pens. Plows, carts, harrows, and sleighs are stored under the awning.

If a house has only one "shell" (*srub*), which is most often the case, then the owner also has a shed or small cabin for storing grain, flour, clothing, footwear, his wife's trunks, and other household items. These sheds or barns are quadrangular structures

This picture of a brick masonry home was taken by the author, Olga Semyonova, presumably in the village of Muraevnia. Noted the covered yard to the left and the trees screening the house, which are included in her written description. From *Rossiia, Polnoe geograficheskoe opisanie*, vol. 2, p. 179.

measuring eight to sixteen feet on a side. They have small windows facing the main house, which is to say the street, for sheds are normally erected opposite the houses so that a row of houses and a row of sheds define a street. In front of the sheds and the houses, willow trees are planted as a fire-safety measure, and a village constable makes sure the peasants maintain this foliage. The willows can reach considerable size and lend a very picturesque aspect to some villages. Inside the sheds, benches line the walls, and shelves are fitted above the benches. Peasants sleep in the sheds during the spring, summer, and fall. For ordinary peasants, these sheds, or small barns, are usually clay-walled, although some log structures also exist, while the rich peasants known as kulaks build masonry sheds and outfit them with metal roofs and iron-plated doors.

Vegetable patches and threshing barns are located behind the yards. A village constable enforces an ordinance requiring that threshing barns be at least two hundred feet away from the houses and, again, surrounded by willows. Like the houses, threshing barns are covered with thatched roofs; the roof framing, however, is supported by studs rather than by rafters as in a house. The threshing goes on in the threshing barns in the winter, and also in the summer during rainy weather. You enter the barn through a gate, which when closed leaves the inside very dark. In the summer, to avoid flies, peasants sleep on the straw floor of the threshing barn.

Every house has an outdoor cellar that is constructed nearby and has a thatched gable roof. A door and a flight of stairs lead inside. A cellar is used for storage of milk, radishes, beets, cabbage, pickled apples, and salted beef.

In winter, if it is cold in the pens outside, the sheep are kept in the main house, as are the cows and pigs that have given birth, along with their calves and piglets. Chickens make their winter roost under the awning in the yard.

[Fire was a great scourge of Russian villages, and arsonists were punished harshly.] Peasants prefer to deal with arsonists themselves. If peasants catch an arsonist in the act, they beat him so brutally that within a few hours he is dead. This fall, a man who had allegedly set fire to the same village six times in the course of the year but was never caught in the act was found in a ravine with his head smashed in. Considering the horror of a village fire, one can understand peasants' rage at arsonists. There is nothing more terrifying than a night fire in a village. I know of cases in which several members of a family perished when they could not get out of a burning house. A lot of livestock is lost in these fires as well. Wattle yards with thatched awnings light up like gunpowder, especially in dry weather, leaving only embers from the animals inside. I myself have seen sheep and pigs, suffocated by smoke, popping inside a burning yard and turning into a charred, shapeless mass. I will never forget one such night when a fire was raging through the peasants' homes and yards, wiping out innocent animals, and in front of a house that had just started to burn lay the emaciated body of a small girl, illuminated by the fire. She had died of diarrhea only hours before the fire started, and her mother had managed to rescue the body from the conflagration.

[At another point in her notes, Semyonova tells of an arsonist who was treated differently. Apparently his act did not have devastating consequences. The punishment of expulsion was nevertheless stern; a peasant without a community is truly an orphan.]

At the peasant assembly of the village of Karavaevo a week ago, an arsonist was expelled from the community. The man in question was a thirty-five-year-old bachelor who had lived with his married elder brother. [This was the second time he was in trouble.] He had already been to prison for another escapade. That occurred when he proposed to a young woman from the same village, with whom he had probably been intimate (but who can know these things for sure?). When she turned him down, he decided to "show" her. One night he got into the storage room in the young woman's home, pulled all of her clothes out of her trunk, and shredded them to pieces. Then he defecated in the trunk. While he was in prison, the woman married another man, and people assure me that it is a good marriage.[3]

Distribution of Property and Duties between the Spouses

The husband owns the house, grain, horses, sheep, and agricultural implements. His funds pay for the house and fenced yard, the main barn, and the threshing barn, and he buys the horses and other livestock, plus wagons and the like. He also buys grain, cereals, beef, cabbage, salt, kerosene ("gas"), and straw for kindling. He is responsible for making bast shoes for the entire family, as well as making ropes and providing everyone with felt boots.

The wife purchases household items, such as bowls, plates, pots, spoons, rolling pins, oven forks, threshing flails, soap, and barrels. From her own supplies of cloth, she makes her husband

3. The man's act was more than vandalism; it was symbolic rape. A woman's trunk is the container for her most cherished (and sometimes only) personal possessions. To enter this container and befoul it as was done here is an act of defilement just short of rape itself.

mittens, scarves, belts, worsted material for his peasant vest (*poddyovka*), and foot cloths (*onuchi*). Men sow flax and women harvest it. The women keep the fiber from the flax crops; the seeds go to the men. Women always try to pick flax while some green is still on it, when the seeds are not yet ripe and the fibers are of better quality. Scutching the flax is usually a woman's job. All the women in a family share the fiber they have picked, dividing it equally in small sheaves. Women always have a need for flax. The amount they pick never seems to be enough, so they try to procure it elsewhere as well. Landlords let peasant women pick flax on the following terms: women pay six to ten rubles to pick a desiatina (2.7 acres) of flax. They scutch the flax and keep the fibers, while the landlord gets the seeds. For this work, a woman normally joins forces with her mother (or with her aunt if her mother is not available). The young woman harvests the plant, and her mother stores it and prepares it for spinning.

A woman also clothes her husband, herself, and their children from head to toe, the only exception being in the case of boots, which the husband makes, or has made, for himself at his own expense. A wife provides her husband with sacking for household needs. In addition, she has to buy with her own money a loom, a spinning wheel and hackle, along with the plank on which a spinner sits and into which a hackle or tow is inserted (*dontse*), and scutches, plus the trunk in which she keeps her personal possessions.

Women's wages are distributed in the following way: during the summer work season, the husband takes the pay for any piecework his wife may do, while she keeps any wages she earns at day labor. In some villages, however, both piecework payments and day-labor wages of a wife are given to her husband. Mowing is also included in the summer work season. For the rest of the year, a woman keeps her wages from both day labor and piecework. Spouses continually argue about work. For example, a husband may have made an agreement with the landlord to mow his hay and haul it to the barn, but his wife balks, claiming that some domestic chore is more important, and the husband has to turn down the job. Sometimes, at the height of the work season when the landlord is prepared to pay high wages for harvesting a crop, all the women refuse to go out and bind sheaves, preferring to stay at home and lie on the stove. "I don't care if my husband loses money, I'm not going to go out binding for him. I've got plenty to do here at home, what with having to clothe him and all." (This gives some idea of the problems a big landlord faces when he has to get a crop in on time in these conditions.)

Theft between the spouses is not uncommon. It may be the husband who steals money from his wife's trunk for some "need" of his or just to enjoy himself at a tavern. Or the wife might take some flour or grain from her husband and use it to pay for soap or some satin cloth at the store. When a husband is drunk, his wife will slip his wallet out of his boot. Children, too, steal eggs or anything handy from their mothers. Wives swipe wool from their husbands.

Pigs are the husband's property, while chickens naturally belong to the wife. The husband takes care of the horse, and the wife tends to the cow. The cow is considered to be a wife's possession, if not quite her property. Such a substantial acquisition as a cow usually requires monetary contributions from both the husband and the wife.

The following practice is common with the cows. Let's say a better-off peasant has a cow and a heifer. When the cow again calves, this heifer is a burden, since the peasant has to feed it. The heifer is therefore given to a poorer peasant on the basis of an oral agreement that he can use the milk of the heifer (as well as of two or three other heifers that he "adopts") until it grows into a cow.[4] The cow is then returned to its owner. If it dies while still in the custody of the poorer peasant, the owner receives the hide. For the

4. Something was apparently lost in the transcription of Semyonova's text at this point. The passage reads literally that the peasant can use the milk from the heifer(s), but as that is clearly impossible (a heifer is a young female cow that has not produced a calf; hence she would not yet be producing milk), she may have meant that the new calf was given to the poor peasant and the cow went with it until the calf was weaned. Possibly, the poor peasant was managing a small herd of heifers, some of which he was breeding, but the first explanation appears more likely, since the Russian seems to refer to the new calf as the one that is a burden.

peasant who has use of the cow, it is known as a "cow out of heifers." Sometimes it happens that toward the end of the period in which the peasant has use of the cow, he will say that he has no cow. [And he might be asked,] "What do you mean, no cow? I saw your wife the other day driving it in from the pasture." "Well, yes, but that's just a cow out of heifers."

The sheep are common property. But sometimes the wife has her own sheep [called *sobinki*, that is, "personal possessions"; they come as a part of her dowry]. If a woman who owns such a sheep dies, her mother gets the animal if she takes the grandchildren in and cares for them. Otherwise, the dead woman's daughter inherits it, but it would never go into the common family property under the control of the husband. When a woman is unable to feed one of her sheep in the winter, she will turn it over temporarily to a poorer peasant, and by way of compensation he keeps the lamb that the sheep delivers in the spring. He, however, is not permitted to take the wool of the sheep.

Wool from the sheep that are common property of the family as a whole is distributed to males and females in a seasonal rotation. Wool shorn in the spring is divided among the women, and wool from the fall shearing goes in equal shares to the men. Sheepskins from the common stock are the property of the men, and they are under no obligation to furnish their wives with winter clothing.

I cannot say that peasants treat their livestock especially well. Horses are routinely beaten. Yet a peasant feels very upset if a horse dies, because this is a great financial loss. A woman reacts the same way to the loss of a cow. When a horse or a cow, or even a sheep, dies, women "wail." In fact, they wail when anything is lost or stolen from their farms. I once heard a peasant woman "wailing" over a pair of half-boots (*koty*) that she lost returning from the fair.

Division of Family Property at Time of Household Partition

Partitions are usually caused by women quarreling about the children—but not always. The head of household may evict one of

A farmyard in the nearby Black Earth province of Tambov. Photo by S. I. Gerasimova from *Rossiia, Polnoe geograficheskoe opisanie,* vol. 2, p.177.

the family members for not contributing enough to the budget. This usually happens when the person in question has a job somewhere else [and is not sending money home]. Sometimes a family just grows so large that it has to break up because of limited space.

When a family decides to arrange a division, they inform the village "elder" (*starosta*), who then calls a meeting of the village council (*skhod*). The role of those present at the meeting is not to determine the distribution of property but merely to evaluate the property and observe the allocation of it, which the family does itself by casting lots. The council also draws up for approval by the township administration an official declaration confirming the distribution of family possessions.

The division proceeds essentially as follows: let's say the entire property has been estimated at 355 rubles 15 kopecks (each item is appraised separately). One party is to receive the house, worth 80 rubles, another party the main barn and the threshing barn, worth 45 and 30 rubles respectively. Lots are cast to see who gets the house, and that party pays the 5-ruble difference to the other party. The rest of the property—buildings, tools, livestock—is likewise divided by casting lots.

When the division is over, the family returns home. After saying a prayer, they cut a loaf of bread in the middle, each party receiving half. If only one or two members move out, they receive not half a loaf but only a slice of bread. This is the source of the expression "a lopped-off piece" [meaning a family member who has voluntarily or forcibly been separated from the household]. After this, both parts of the family kiss goodbye, occasionally crying, and finally part.

Bread plays a central role in the peasant household and in all the events of peasant life. Only in periods of famine and when a priest's visit is expected is bread missing from the shelf. In the first case, it is plainly not available, and in the second, it is removed to safekeeping away from "covetous eyes."

Budget

Here is a budget for a peasant family consisting of six persons: husband, wife, husband's elderly mother, and three children (the eldest of whom is twelve years old). Economically, the family is about average; it owns one horse, one cow, and two sheep.

INCOME (in a good harvest year)

The crop yield from the family's 5.4 acre land allotment[5] is:

Rye	(16 shocks)	= 13 quarters (*chetvert'*)
Oats	(8 shocks)	= 11 quarters
Millet	(4 shocks)	= 3 quarters
Potatoes		= 10 quarters

5. This is the allotment for a family with two adult males (known as "revision souls") listed in the census. [Semyonova]

Out of this sold:

8 quarters 4 measures of oats at 2.40 per quarter	18 Rb 20 k.
Day labor	10 Rb
Piecework	12 Rb
Pay for farming 8.1 acres	15 Rb
Sale of a heifer	10 Rb
Income as a carter in winter	12 Rb
TOTAL	77 Rb 20 k.

Expenses

Grain (seeds for rye, oats, millet, potatoes. The remainder of crops consumed.)

Grain purchased (540 lbs.)	9 Rb
Footwear	10 Rb
Clothing	15 Rb
Kerosene	2 Rb
Matches and salt	2 Rb 30 k.
Meat for the local patron saint's day, Christmas, and Easter	4 Rb
Fish for Shrovetide	2 Rb
Vodka for the patron saint's day and Shrovetide	2 Rb 10 k.
Paid to the priest	1 Rb 85 k.
Fuel (straw) at 50 kopecks per shock	5 Rb
Church donations and candles	3 Rb
Taxes (national, county, township, and village for two male persons)	18 Rb
Zemstvo taxes	5 Rb
Tar	1 Rb 20 k.
Pay to shepherd	1 Rb 20 k.
TOTAL	81 Rb 65 k.

Subsidiary Trades of Peasants

Cottage trades in this region are practiced solely to meet domestic needs and include fulling of felt boots, sewing, shoemaking, carpentry, harnessmaking, thatching roofs, laying brick for houses and stoves, brick baking, and repairing accordions. The people who engage in these activities are also farmers, and so they perform many of these crafts rather poorly. Bricks, for example, are frequently irregular in shape and underbaked. The poor workmanship in this trade may, however, be a result of the fact that this line of work is relatively new here. It was only in the 1870s that bricks began to replace logs in the construction of peasant homes. On the other hand, the peasants have perfected the techniques for

[Prices of some goods and services:]

Felt boots (man)	from 80 k. to 1 Rb
(woman)	50 k.–60 k.
Undercoat (adult)	75 k.–1 Rb
(child)	40 k.–50 k.
Fur coat (man)	1 Rb–1 Rb 30 k.
(woman)	80 k.–1 Rb
Low fur-trimmed boots	2 Rb 50 k.
Shoes	3 Rb
Boots	7 Rb 50 k.
Construction of a log house	15 Rb (with benches and table)
" hallway	5 Rb
" floor or ceiling	3 Rb
" brick house	15 Rb
" brick stove	3 Rb–4 Rb
Thatch a barn	7 Rb–11 Rb
" a house	3 Rb
" a yard	8 Rb–10 Rb
Repair an accordion	10 Rb
Caulk a house	1 Rb
Wattle a fence	5 Rb
" a hallway	2 Rb
Window frame	40 k.–70 k.
Door	80 k.–1 Rb
Timber for a house	35 Rb
Bricks (1,000)	4 Rb 50 k.–10 Rb

thatching roofs. Ditch digging, too, is well developed. In some counties, the entire male population of certain villages hire themselves out as ditch diggers. They work in artels[6] and sometimes contract jobs far away from home. Carpenters also sometimes work in artels. In some villages women make lace.

[As in other societies, in peasant Russia some trades were respected more than others. A few were contemned. Semyonova mentions one of these: flayers.]

Flayers are peasants who strip the skin from dead or slaughtered animals. Peasants believe it to be an "unclean" occupation—so much so that others will not eat food from the same dish as a flayer.[7] Flayers are also subjected to jokes and mockery. Every village has from two to four flayers among the peasants. Flaying a cow or a horse costs thirty to forty kopecks. Those who resort to this occupation are usually poor peasants, but some flayers are cripples, the simple-minded, and improvident landless men.

Terms of Payment for Work

The phrase "Taking an advance payment from a landlord or merchant for future work" can describe the undertaking of a peasant family to sow and harvest from five to sixteen acres for a landlord in both the spring field and the winter field. A contract is drawn up to this effect and notarized at the township supervisor's office. After this, a peasant receives in advance the entire sum for the work to be performed. If paid for in advance, the plowing, sowing, weeding, and harvesting of a crop cost the landlord from four and a half to five and a half rubles per desiatina [2.7 acres], whereas the same work will cost him from seven to twelve rubles if payment is made upon completion. Some landlords exploit peasants terribly by means of these advance payments. Yet peasants submit to this

6. An artel is "a cooperative association of workers or craftsmen working together by agreement, under the guidance of an elected head." *Dictionary of Russian Historical Terms from the Eleventh Century to 1917*, comp. Sergei G. Pushkarev, ed. George Vernadsky and Ralph T. Fisher, Jr. (New Haven: Yale University Press, 1970), 2.

7. "Unclean" here has the special meaning of an association with unclean spirits, that is, evil.

form of enslavement in order to pay taxes. They contract for the advance payments at just the time taxes come due: the months from August through December. [See "Form of a Contract between Seasonal Employers and Peasants" in the appendix.]

Payments to the Priest[8]

1. Wedding: six rubles cash, three bottles of vodka (fifty-five kopecks per bottle), two pounds of pretzels, a chicken, bread, and pies. For lighting of the chandelier and other candles in the church, about two rubles. This provides a "first-class wedding."

2. Baptism: fifty kopecks, plus bread.

3. Funeral: three rubles (but if candle holders and a high-quality shroud are used, the price could go as high as eight rubles). Funeral for a child: seventy-five kopecks.

4. Office for the dead: ten kopecks.

5. Special mass: two rubles.

6. Confession: from five to twenty kopecks (as you wish).

7. Extreme unction: one and a half rubles (with candles).[9]

8. Prayers requested by the commune for rain: three or four rubles.

9. [This number is skipped in the document]

10. Cleansing ritual against mice: thirty to fifty kopecks. If a mouse falls into a tub of pickles, sauerkraut, or pickled apples, the woman of the house will nearly always summon the priest to perform a cleansing ritual. The mouse is plucked from the tub, and the priest proceeds to say a prayer over the tub, pass a cross over it three times, and then bite into a pickle or apple or try some of the sauerkraut. After this, the contents of the tub are again regarded as clean. (A mouse, to the peasants' way of thinking, is "foul" and "polluting" [*nechist'*].)

8. The following material is from Semyonova's archive in AGO, f. 109, op. 1, d. 170, ch. 5, ll. 26-28.

9. This sacrament for Russians is not granted solely to a dying person but can also be used as an aid in the recovery of someone who is injured or ill.

12. Communal prayer for Easter: one ruble. The priest makes the rounds of his parishioners with a public prayer (that is, a collection) five times a year. At Easter, he receives forty-five kopecks, bread, and a pie from each household and an egg from each individual. At Christmas, he gets fifteen kopecks and a pie; at Epiphany, twenty-five kopecks, bread, and a pie; on the tsarist holy day, twenty kopecks, bread, and a pie; and at St. Nicholas Day in the spring,[10] fifteen kopecks and a pie. It is typical that the collection for St. Nicholas Day, which was instituted fifteen years ago to pay for the restoration of the fence around the churchyard, was subsequently kept by the priest for himself. The money is divided among the priest and the other clerical staff, while the householders themselves distribute the offerings of bread by mutual agreement to the priest, the deacon, and the sub-deacon. The clergy normally use the bread collected at Easter as food for their horses. The bread is dried into hardtack and then softened in water when fed to the livestock. The eggs, which are hard-boiled, are salted and used by the priest to feed his farmhand (peasants do not like these salted eggs).

Some priests simply go right up and take bread off the shelf in a peasant home, saying: "Well, I guess you baked that bread for me, didn't you?" This is the reason the peasants hide their bread from the priest's prying eyes.

When a peasant owes a debt to the clergy, the priest puts pressure on him to pay as the opportunity presents itself, especially at weddings: "Pay me what you owe, and then I'll do the wedding; otherwise I won't do it." And, indeed, he will refuse to do it. In one village in which the priest is adamant about debts, I know several instances in which his refusal to perform a marriage ceremony has led to cohabitation by unwed couples. In some villages, the clergy organizes obligatory memorial services (every Saturday), for which they exact one ruble a year per household. For entering a marriage in the official records of vital events (*metrika*),

10. St. Nicholas, the most popular saint of Russia, also has a holy day in the winter.

the priest takes two and a half rubles; this is paid by the bride. The groom pays for the wedding itself.[11]

Peasants consider a priest to be a sponger: "He just stands there, reads a prayer, and you have to give him a fifty-kopeck piece."

As for witchcraft and goblins, werewolves, and the like, they are believed in least by the very persons who are considered to be sorcerers and witches, the peasants who do cures by reciting incantations and such. "Witchcraft" is a fairly lucrative occupation, and it is amusing to observe how a clever witch "acts out her role" in the village. I wish I could listen in when two "witches" were having a conversation and did not have to pretend in front of each other.

We have a witch like that in our village, a really audacious one, and it has occurred to me more than once that she might look upon the parish priest as her colleague, a fellow professional.

Religion[12]

When the tsar was ill, the peasants asked me what he was suffering from, inquiring with some interest but also with complete equanimity. "You see, there he is the tsar and all; no one escapes illness. Of course, they have to go and call in the doctors." (A clear note of mistrust toward doctors can be heard in this statement.) "Hear tell he's not in Piter but at his country estate; if he dies there, won't they be taking him, just as they did with his father, into Piter for burial?" "They said mass for the tsar—the priest was saying that they prayed for the tsar." All this, I repeat, is said with complete composure in the course of the peasants' daily chores.

11. Here ends the unpublished entry beginning with "Payments to the Priest."
12. Most of the section that follows from here to the last two paragraphs of the chapter was not published in the 1914 edition of Semyonova's work but is excerpted in Varvara Shneider's eulogy. Shneider, "Pamiati Ol'gi Petrovny Semenovoi," 59-61. Six sentences from the 1914 work are, however, woven into the third paragraph of this section.

They speak with much greater animation about some wedding scandal in a nearby village. The tsar is far away—"at the other end of the earth," off in a fog.

I have sometimes thought that a belief in the tsar, a belief that he is here in existence somewhere, ought to lend support to the peasants' belief in God. For a peasant the tsar is as far away as God, and his existence is beyond question; so the existence of God, too, ought to seem more certain than it does to us [educated people].

The peasant God is something material, very much so, in fact. He is the giver of rain, of drought, health, and sickness. The tsar is a provider in case of need perhaps, the defender of our borders, of our land, which feeds the peasant. Among the mass of peasants, there is nothing mystical about their relationship to the tsar or to God, just as there is nothing mystical about their idea of an afterlife. They simply give no thought to an afterlife, just as they give no thought to the coming year. It is amazing how essentially irreligious they are! It is only the old people when their health is failing who exhibit a confused fear in the face of "the life beyond the grave." Here we see an ordinary association of their physical pain with what they assume will be the physical sufferings of hell. Can they really be considered Russian Orthodox? Not at all. They are confused, helpless, and terrified, and have no idea of what to do "to gain salvation." "Who knows," they say, "maybe the Freemasons or the Molokane [sectarians known as 'milk drinkers'] have a better way to achieve salvation!" How timid, uncertain, and full of doubt is this statement, uttered by gasping and coughing old folks!

Both heaven and hell are understood purely in material terms. In hell people suffer physically for their sins, and in heaven their goodness is rewarded obviously with apples (although the Molokane sect believes that heaven is a place where people sing hymns to God). You only have to recall the usual formula in folktale references to heaven: "and he found himself in a Garden of Eden; the trees were leafy and green and heavy with apples." The apple is the favorite peasant delicacy. People associate the idea of apples with something that does not demand the kind of heavy labor that growing grain does. Real paradise is a place where people do not have to sow and reap by the sweat of their brows.

It is said that our people cannot imagine a person "without God." Perhaps it is so. I have heard peasants pose the question about many upper-class people who do not go to church: "What faith do they practice?" "Don't they have their God?" The [sectarians known as] Flagellants have "their God." [In reference to people with a good standard of living, they might say:] "Look how wealthy they are; He must give them that." The word "give" is the crux of the matter, it seems to me. Every person needs his or her God as a personal benefactor.

It is in the notions associated with the land, with Moist Mother Earth, that you find the mystical side of the peasants. Here you see the residue of their ancient, separate worldview, which alas is much more deeply felt and poetic than our vaunted Russian Orthodoxy. Here are also the affecting "Radiant Sun," "Bright Moon," "Valiant Charger–Faithful Steed,"[13] plus vivid and touching images of communion with nature, human sorrow, and orphanhood. It is not God whom the orphan girl asks to resurrect her parents so that they can give her their blessing as she goes off to be married, but instead Moist Mother Earth to whom she appeals to raise her mother from the grave. And, of course, Orthodoxy does not conform especially well to the peasant soul. And what is it that the peasant lacks in this regard? An awareness of his sinfulness is inborn in him. There is also a "spiritual thirst" (which you see expressed at least in the church schisms), but he has not one iota, and nowhere to obtain it, of any kind of "platonic" attachments or "platonic" interests. These are the conditions in which he exists, and is this not then the reason for his undisciplined behavior and drunkenness, the senseless daring of the young men (the "able-bodied" draftees, for example), and other such manifestations?

13. It is impossible to render adequately the sense of these poetic images from ancient Russian epic tales, the first two of which also appear as personifications referring to individual heroes.

[As for the peasants' ideas about who is just and who will attain salvation,][14] whether it is the poor people or the rich people, he will say that in most cases "the just" are the old people, and definitely not the rich. Yet it is harder for these just people to win salvation than it is for the rich. Merchants, for example, can always bequeath their money to the church or leave funds at a number of monasteries for prayers to be said in their memory, and in this manner "save their souls" and enter into heaven. In regard to life on earth, the poor "just" people are, of course, better.

The peasants hold to the notion that the Last Judgment will take three days. On the first day, the Lord will judge the monks and priests, on the second, the nobility and merchants, and on the third, the peasants. (Antichrist will be born on the fourth day. He will lure the people with promises of "food, clothing, and shoes.") In general, peasants are impressed most by what is written in the Gospels about the Last Judgment, and their thoughts dwell mainly on that. "Oh," they say, "how terrifying it will be!"

14. The following two paragraphs come from Semyonova's field notes in Arkhiv AN SSSR, f. 906, op. 1, d. 26, l. 307.

9

❖❖❖

PEASANT IDEALS, WORK HABITS, AND CAUSES OF POVERTY

The Russian village was changing. Contact with the big city was becoming the common experience of many villagers, as the first vignette in this chapter makes clear. It also reveals two of the characteristics Semyonova thought that she could discern in the peasant way of thinking. The first is a very short time horizon, the inability of the peasant to project plans and expectations far into the future. Nothing could be counted on, not even the ordinary expectation in modern society that most children will reach adulthood. The second is the lack of interest in saving money. This characteristic is related to the first; if there is no future, at least none that can be counted on and into which one can project hopes and plans, then why sacrifice anything for it? It makes more sense to work only as much as necessary to make it through the current year and to consume whatever extra comes one's way.

Semyonova believed that one reason for the lack of motivation to save was the impossibility of doing so in the face of price fluctuations that ate up profits in a good year. Yet while making this point, she seems to want to identify a deeper cause for this peasant attitude in the experience of several centuries of serfdom. Unfortunately, she fails to define exactly what she means by this.

Semyonova saw a large difference between the notions of private property and theft in peasant society and in educated

Russian society. The peasants' ideas about theft seem again to have been associated with their negative attitudes toward saving for the future. Objects taken for immediate consumption were not regarded as stolen. An important element here is, of course, also the source of the appropriated goods; the property of a landlord or the government was evidently considered in some larger sense everyone's property. But we should not draw too sharp a distinction here, because Semyonova also points out that peasants stole from one another.

What did Semyonova consider the source of these attitudes she believed were characteristic of the peasants: their lack of respect for the property of others, failure to invest in the future, and disinterest in hard work? Semyonova does not offer an explicit explanation or analysis. But in her notes about the conversations and hopes of the peasants, their difficulties in paying their taxes and in making money even in a good harvest year, and the constraints that joint responsibility[1] *and other institutions of peasant life placed on enterprise, she seems to imply that the peasants' attitudes were related to the problem of land. Most peasants did not have a piece of land they could call their own and in which it would make sense to invest, though this is something they obviously wished to have. Keep in mind, too, the larger frame of reference that I outlined in the introduction to this book for possibly understanding their behavior: the notion that the peasants thought in terms of "limited good" and the consequent bias against accumulation.*

But before too hastily accepting the views of Semyonova, we should consider the likelihood that peasants used means other than setting aside money to save and invest. I have already mentioned more than once the importance of symbolic capital. In this chapter, we can glimpse another, more

1. "Joint responsibility" is a Russian practice of very long standing, and a difficult one to explain briefly. In essence, it meant that all members of a group (an artel or village commune, for example) stood surety for all other members in dealings contracted by (or imposed upon) the group as whole.

material form of investment: livestock holdings. In her description of tax collection and arrears, Semyonova refers to peasant families that were able to pay their taxes and still maintain herds of sufficient size to render inconspicuous extra animals left with them by relatives. Some other families were apparently willing to risk tax penalties to maintain their investments in livestock. For the majority, however, the few animals they owned were probably essential to their farming operations and did not represent savings.

PYOTR IS A rather simple-hearted and plain-looking peasant twenty-eight to thirty years old who owns his own household apart from his parents and brothers. My question takes him aback.

I: "Tell me, Pyotr, do you ever think about the time your boys will be grown-up and married, and how you and your wife will run the house together with your sons and daughters-in-law?"

Pyotr thought for a moment and replied artlessly: "No, I guess I don't."

"Honestly?"

"I'd think about it, if somehow I could really count on it happening. Of course, there would be a change, my sons would be relieving me—but, look, I really can't be sure of any of that. So what's the point of thinking about it? Do you really think they will grow up? They could just as easily die first. . . . I think it is probably more likely that they will die."

"Pyotr, have you ever planned to go to Moscow? Did you ever want to do that?"

"I was planning to go three years ago, but my mother wouldn't let me."

"Just look how eager peasants are to go there nowadays. I often wonder what attracts you people there. Can it be that life is better there? The people who go don't bring back much money. But could things be better even so? And what a lot of liquor!"

"Of course, we drink a lot there. Hardly anyone brings money back home. You're right about that. Sometimes a peasant sends his son to Moscow, and the fellow will send some money home on occasion, especially if he's afraid of his father, but he'll never bring anything back. But not everyone is a drunkard."

"True. But what is there for those who do not drink? I believe that by now the young men all know that you can't get rich there."

Pyotr, giving the question some thought, replies:

"It seems to me that many of them go there for clothes, too. Here you go around in the same old rags winter and summer, but in town you can get decent clothes and shoes. Why, the way they look when they come back from town, we can't even stand next to them." (Indeed, it is a matter of honor for a young man to return from town to his village looking like "a Moscow dandy," sporting a vest, a jacket, galoshes, and even slacks.)

I: "Did you really want to go to Moscow, then? Are you sorry you weren't able to get there?"

Pyotr (smiling quietly): "I wanted to, of course. Even now I sometimes want to go there, especially when one of the fellows comes back with a lot of good stories. I get envious. But when I don't hear anything about Moscow, I all but forget that the place exists. I just go on living and don't give it a thought."

"So, what do they tell about Moscow?"

"They say the pay is good there, and people dress better, and there is plenty of everything—tea, liquor, food—not like here in the village. The pay is high, and lots of everything, they say."

A peasant's ideal is to be near a warm stove and have at least an hour to himself. Sometimes the ideal is associated with the city life of a carter or a janitor, but again not with the idea of saving money. City life appears attractive because in Moscow one can spend the whole day in a tavern; "drinking there is more fun," and "the food is better there," they will say. While a young man may send something to his parents back home (albeit usually only after many entreaties), a newlywed peasant who has moved out of his

Peasant man making barrel hoops on a cooper's bench. Riazan province. Courtesy of the Riazan Museum.

Interior of a typical peasant home, featuring the large Russian stove. Watercolor by an unknown Russian artist. Courtesy of David L. Ransel.

parents' home and become a household head on his own will most likely (there are exceptions, of course) return from the big city "as poor as a church mouse," with only memories of food and drink to savor.

You might say that the peasants *never* have any money.[2] When they sell their grain in the fall, they have to "deal with taxes" and get the larder stocked for the winter. Then the fall festival of their patron saint approaches, and all the money is spent. When sons and brothers send money from Moscow or when peasants get some money from off-farm work, again "it goes to taxes," or to a holiday celebration or a wedding. Generally speaking, it goes where money is needed and is thus once again spent up. Your average peasant is not used to having extra cash around, and so he quickly drinks up what little extra money has come his way. He looks on this extra as if it were purely happenstance, as if it had just fallen out of the sky; and so it gets drunk up. A man's wallet is known as a *gomonok* [a slang word meaning something like "the last abode of money," from the Russian *ugomon dlia deneg*].

Peasants believe that "it is a sin to pile up money." Savings are just one more stone around a sinner's neck. At present, it is difficult to tell if their utter indifference to the future actually rests on beliefs such as these or if they "dredge up" these ideas in order to justify their predicament to themselves and their families. Probably both factors are at work here.

The cost of cabbage varies from one ruble per hundred in a normal year to three rubles in a good harvest year. A suckling pig starts at seventy kopecks but rises to three rubles in a good year. The range for apples is from fifty kopecks to two rubles. The prices are set by sellers and producers (owners of vegetable gardens and leaseholders of orchards). These price ranges reflect the increase in peasants' expenses in a good year. Yet, people seem to believe that

2. This paragraph is inserted from Semyonova's field notes in Arkhiv AN SSSR, f. 906, op. 1, d. 26, l. 335.

peasants can "save" when there is a good harvest! Irrespective of the actual situation, however, peasants give no thought to saving for the future. If a peasant has a good harvest that will keep him until the next year, he will stay at home and loaf and cannot be enticed to take an extra job at any price. Peasants hire themselves out as farm laborers only when driven to it by dire need, when they have, so to speak, a knife at their throat. [Then they will do] the most arduous work imaginable.

You really ought to see the arrogance, even impudence, with which a ragged laborer will go to his employer in a good year and ask to settle up before the end of the agreed-upon work period: "Be so kind as to pay up!"

Landlord: "What's wrong? Are you saying that you're treated badly here?"

"Nothing's wrong. I just don't want to stay here anymore. I'm going home."

"I can't let you go. The work season is just starting. I'm not going to give you any money. I need to harvest my crops, too; that's what I hired you for."

"If you don't pay, I'll leave anyway."

If the landlord does not let him go, he will work very poorly on purpose, damage equipment, water the horses to the point that they get sick, and the like.

"How come the landlord did not want to let you go at first, and then he kicked you out?"

Ivan (with a smirk): "Well, I just goofed off instead of working, so he let me go."

They really do abandon their jobs as farm laborers and in their bast shoes and rags go and harvest their own crops, after which they climb up on the stove and seem not to need a thing except bread, warmth, and a "missus" they can order around.

Yet when there is nothing to eat and no fuel to heat the house, these same peasants will go to a landlord and grovel in order to get work. "I'll do any kind of job you have; just take me and my missus." "You can pay us in bread, just enough to get us through the winter." They bow clear to the ground, even shed tears.

Until recently, some peasants could not distinguish one type of paper money from another, count money correctly, or figure out the prices for manufactured goods. But now every peasant has a billfold, and he knows how to manage properly his tax records (*podatnaia knizhka*) and to calculate his accounts with the landlord or storekeeper. Moreover, he has learned the value of his own labor and, knowing that merchants like to overcharge him and landowners try to take advantage of his poverty and hire him for low wages, he in turn has mastered various ruses to work less and charge more for his labor. If he thinks that a landowner is offering him too little for a job, he would rather forget the work and stay home, taking comfort in the thought that the landlord will eventually have to pay someone else even more.

The Peasants' Attitudes to Noble and Merchant Landlords[3]

In the depths of the peasants' souls, it seems to me, they prefer landowners from the nobility. They probably feel and understand that noble landowners "in general" treat them more humanely and better. Peasants are not averse to taking advantage of "good-hearted" noble landlords, not to mention that they always expect to receive a handout from them.

The peasants will sometimes come to an inexperienced noble landowner, hang around by the porch hemming and hawing, and, having accepted some medicine or other, will say straight out: "Would you be so good as to give us some [monetary] aid?" On occasion, they will make up a story about how poor they are in order to receive a little larger handout. More than once I have observed a noble landlady in these situations. She was well aware of these at times naive lies, and yet not deterred by them from taking pity on a peasant and freely giving him assistance. In such a case, not a single "Ivan" would have understood that the woman saw through his lie and only out of a sense of pity looked beyond it

3. The following material is drawn from excerpts of Semyonova's notes published in the eulogy by Varvara Shneider, "Pamiati Ol'gi Petrovny Semenovoi," 54-56.

and gave him assistance. On the contrary, any peasant would have been convinced that he had outwitted the wealthy person. Ivan, of course, would not have suffered any pangs of conscience on this account, since he would figure that rich people earn their salvation by such acts of charity (there is a folktale about a housekeeper who deceived her noble master into benefiting the poor and in this way saved his soul). Besides all this, peasants tend to regard noble landlords and their managerial abilities with scorn and have no faith whatsoever in them.

As for merchant landowners, the peasants have great respect for their ability to realize a solid return from agriculture, and they admire their industrious management of the farm and the fact that the merchants give attention to everything. In this connection, how a merchant runs his business, how he is able to catch workers stealing things from him, and the like are frequent topics of conversation among peasants. By the same token, peasants do not like merchants, of course, and they deal with them in their own firm and familiar way. Nowadays, for example, when fellows use the formal "you" in addressing even young peasant women, the villagers usually continue to use the informal "you" with merchants and to respond to a merchant's swearing with an equal amount of their own, reminding him that "you're no better than the rest of us," you are no noble. Naturally, if the peasants think they can get something out of a merchant, they will humble themselves before him even more than they would before a noble landlord (some merchants love to have the peasants genuflect before them). But the people least liked by the peasants are the noble landlords who manage their estates tightfistedly like kulaks (*kulakovatye dvoriane*). The peasants forgive them nothing and will burn them out and take vengeance on them for any reason, so long as they do not fear their ties to the authorities. In the moments when peace reigns between the peasants and such a kulak, it is a rare peasant who does not think or say that a noble is not supposed to be involved in all the ins and outs of his business. So the mental outlook of Ivan is rather complex. On the one hand, he lacks respect for the noble because of his inability to master agriculture and toil on the land as the peasant does; on the other, [he appreciates] the grandeur of the noble. There is obviously a peasant aesthetic conception that opposes the noble to the merchant and muzhik moiling in dung. The religious sectarians envy the freedom of nobles to devote their time to thoughts about salvation, a kind of freedom not enjoyed by them, peasants who constantly have to worry about earning their daily bread amid the miserable conditions of village life. The sectarians talk about this openly. In the view of the peasants, this is the real meaning of being wealthy: that you do not have to count pennies or sully your noble dignity by bothering with the minutiae of your farm operations—and it is, incidentally, much more advantageous for "Ivan" if he has this kind of landlord.[4]

Walking down the village street, I see a wagon loaded with cabbage standing near a poor little house. The horse has been unharnessed and taken inside the fence. While the owner of the home leans idly on the front end of the wagon, three women are busy picking out the best cabbage heads and peeling loose leaves off of them. Two tiny girls, around four years old, carry the cleaned cabbage heads into the open door of the barn and arrange them on the earthen floor, work that has been going on now for about two hours. All this time the man has just stood there, only occasionally bestirring himself to roll a cigarette. The women talk among themselves, sometimes in rapid high voices and sometimes in an unhurried drawl, about the quality of the cabbage and its high price; even so, they work rather fast. But you should see the little girls! What diligence, speed, and determination they display in carrying the cabbage to the storage room! How eager they are for their mother or aunt to pass them a cabbage head, and how radiant are their dirty little faces as they toddle barefoot to the storage room with a head of cabbage or even two heads! One of the women goes into the house and returns carrying in her arms a boy of two and a half. At first he screws up his eyes against the sun; then, with a

4. Here ends the section excerpted from Shneider's eulogy.

Peasant girls from the village of Kultuki, Kasimov district of Riazan province. Courtesy of the Riazan Museum.

serious expression, he observes the girls for a few moments, and finally struggles to get down. On still-shaky legs, he approaches the wagon and amusingly grabs at the air with his hands to get a cabbage, saying: "Mama, give me one!" His mother is reluctant at first, and the boy starts crying. "All right, all right, take it; just keep quiet." The boy now beams and, his eyes not yet dry, joins the girls in carrying heads of cabbage to the storage room. "Just look at them," one woman remarks, "you can't drive them away from work. But wait till they grow up; you won't be able to make them work with a stick. That's the way it always is." Maybe this is because for a three-year-old Ivan, the experience with cabbage, as with other objects and people around him, is new, while a fifteen-year-old boy is accustomed to the drab routine. Or perhaps the apathy, gloom, and indifference that will accompany him till his last hour result from his diet of potatoes and stale bread? At any rate, the difference between a three-year-old Ivan and a fifteen-year-old one is enormous.

The peasants' lack of respect for hard work is remarkable. "Him? He digs in the field like a beetle from morning till night!" They often say this with scorn.

Could it be that this attitude reflects unpleasant memories of obligatory labor services under serfdom, and that the desire to stay home and loaf, thinking, "At least I can take this one day for myself," is just a natural reaction?

[A peasant woman was hired to cook for our farm laborers.] She took some of the flour she was given for making bread for the workers and used it to bake some cakes for herself. She planned to secretly "gorge" herself and her farm laborer husband on them, but the village elder found her out and reported to me. (The woman was not subjected to any punishment other than a reprimand.) I talked about this incident with another woman, also a house servant.

I: "How do you like what Akulina did?"

Katerina is uneasy at first, then blurts out: "Well, I think Mitrii [the elder] was a fool to bother you with such trifles. Big deal, a woman baked some bread for herself and ate it."

I: "But she stole the flour for it."

Katerina: "That's not stealing! She just baked and ate it. She didn't take the cakes to her room or hide them in the storeroom."

I: "But she took the flour, and as a result the laborers had less bread. What's the difference if she stole it and took it home or ate it right here? It's still robbery."

Katerina: "But she ate the cakes right here in your house, together with her husband; that's not robbery. If she had stolen the flour from a locked cupboard or saved it for the future, that would probably be a sin."

Try as I might to explain to Katerina that unauthorized appropriation of another person's property, whether consumed immediately or saved for future use, is still a theft, she would not agree with me.

The very same elder who turned in Akulina, when he is guarding the landlord's apple trees against raids by the boys hired on temporarily as shepherds, fills his pockets with apples every time he makes the rounds.

Property that belongs to the state is treated with even less respect than that of a landlord. Peasants reason that "the tsar has plenty of everything," and they steal whatever they can get their hands on. It seems impossible to protect the state forest, however many the number of foresters and guards.

I have observed that peasants, either out of habit or perhaps from some genetic predisposition, have a deep affection for the land. At any rate, a majority of peasants (even those who have lived in town) envy landowners more than anything else. Peasants regard "capital" [money] as more precarious than land; it can slip from your hands much faster because of the temptations to which it exposes its owner. One of the most deep-rooted and firm convictions among peasants is that one day all the land will become theirs. It is terribly amusing to observe how clever they can sometimes be in avoiding this issue in their conversations with landlords. As for the landlords, older peasants consider them to be "weaklings" or "softies," who squander their capital because they are unable to do hard work. It is hard to tell if the younger generation will adopt this view. It seems to me that these young people (I refer here to eighteen-to-twenty-year-old males) have no definite views. They have discarded many of the old verities but have not yet found anything with which to replace them. Perhaps this is because young people still depend on their parents and have not had to go it on their own.

The conversations of peasant men do not stray far from their domestic affairs, field work, taxes, the township council, and the like. Sometimes they talk about other things, for example, the special favors they expect on the occasion of a tsarist coronation or the birth of an heir to the throne. They naturally hope for an exemption from tax arrears. When parish schools first opened, the men spoke of its being done on the initiative of the new tsaritsa [Alexandra, wife of Nicholas II], for when she married the tsar, it is said, she poked fun at him because of the backwardness of his people. Rumor has it that the tsaritsa is "kind," and peasants tend to think that she "may have some additional favors in store for them." Any favor from the tsar provokes speculation about the possibility of more benefits to come.

Women, of course, almost never participate in these conversations. They normally engage in gossip about neighbors or about the families of the local landlords and their household staffs.

Tax collection, too, provokes much grumbling on the part of the peasants. "Does the tsar really not have enough money? We have so little land, and yet have to pay high taxes," one peasant will say. Another might respond with a common adage such as: "It's not the tsar who taxes us but his servants. It's not the tsar who runs things but the huntsman."[5] The peasants frequently talk among themselves about this issue and express their envy of the

5. The word in Russian is *psar'*, the man who handles the dogs during a hunt, and probably refers metaphorically to government officials, who the peasants assume act on behalf of the large landowners.

powerful landlords. In the early 1880s, persistent rumors circulated in the village about a possible reallocation of the large landed estates to the peasants.

Peasants also complain a lot about the practice of making each villager responsible for the obligations of all other villagers [the "joint responsibility" custom referred to earlier]. "We had two brothers in our village, both of them drunks, who lived with their elderly father. They accumulated arrears in excess of 150 rubles. Last spring they both died, and their debt was laid on the rest of us—and besides that, we had to support their father. As you know, our village is small, only fifteen families. Why do I have to pay for a drunk? What kind of justice is that? There's no justice in our village." Almost every peasant has a similar tale.

The better-off peasants are bitter about the attitude of their poorer neighbors. "They hate and envy us constantly, saying things like: 'What makes you think you're so much better? Just wait, you're going to be as poor as us.' If you plant an apple tree, they resent it, saying: 'Now that big shot is planting an orchard! We are starving while he is putting in an orchard, and fencing it off at that!'" And they think nothing of breaking down the fence and uprooting the tree. If the tree happens to survive and bear fruit, they feel it is their duty to raid it. "That's how much hate they have! And if some misfortune should befall you, they'll make sure to finish you off." The well-to-do peasant who recited this lament came into his money by pure chance and is not the kind of person who takes advantage of his neighbors' poverty to improve his own lot. This farmer harvests up to 120 shocks of rye off the plot he leases (landlords lease out the land to peasants for seven to twelve rubles per desiatina a year) and is familiar with horticulture because he worked as a gardener for twenty years. Yet, despite great efforts, he had not been able to develop either an orchard or a vegetable garden. "I tried and tried, but now," he said with a dismissive wave of his hand, "I've abandoned the idea and just buy produce." Arson motivated by revenge is [also] very frequent.

When tax collections begin in September, the kulaks [rich peasants] rejoice. If the ordinary peasants are not prompt with their taxes, the authorities first jail the elders of the communities that are in arrears. Then the elders see to it that those failing to pay up are themselves put in jail. The ultimate measure is auctioning the livestock of a defaulter. Occasionally, because of the practice of joint responsibility, the authorities do not bother to check who paid taxes and who did not: the auction simply starts with the first house at the edge of the village. But if they are prosecuting only the families that have not paid up, these defaulters try to protect their livestock by hiding it on the property of their rich relatives who have paid the tax.

The sale is normally carried out by the township supervisor, with the district police officer (*stanovoi*) occasionally present. Women "wail" when their cattle are sold. The auction prices are naturally lower than normal market prices. A cow or a horse that is worth thirty rubles is sold for only ten or fifteen rubles. The principal buyers are kulaks. The peasants who lose their livestock do whatever they can to get it back. They pawn their clothes and those of their wives, and may sell their spring fields as cheaply as ten rubles per desiatina to the very same kulaks who have taken possession of their livestock. When such a peasant family scrapes together enough money, they buy back their cow or horse, overpaying as much as five rubles; if their horse was auctioned for ten rubles, they now have to pay fifteen rubles to get it back. When kulaks purchase a spring field from a needy peasant, they allow him a "grace period" of one month during which he still can buy his field back, but, again, only with an overpayment of up to five rubles per desiatina. One might want to think of the five rubles as an interest charge, but this is not the case, since the sale and repurchase are two separate transactions. The very same kulak may lend money to peasants at a low rate of interest or even interest-free. If a peasant treats the kulak to drinks, the kulak will lend him money for a period of time with no interest. If the peasant cannot pay up at the time agreed upon, a bottle of vodka is all it takes to have the kulak extend the date of payment.

There was an article in *Novoe Vremia* magazine about the inequitable taxation of peasants. The author calculated that in Central Russia a family of five pays approximately nine rubles a year in state taxes, while a family of the same size living in Siberia pays only half that amount. The article is titled "The Impoverishment of the Central Regions," and the author regards the main cause of this impoverishment as the unequal allocation of the tax burden between the center and the periphery.

But what about the many other reasons for the peasants' destitution? I already mentioned the price fluctuations on basic necessities. Even a shoemaker's prices vary from seven rubles for a pair of boots in a bad harvest year to ten rubles in a good year. Furthermore, enormous amounts are squandered in taverns. I know a family in which the husband, after selling grain in town for twenty rubles, never comes back home with more than fourteen or fifteen rubles in his pocket. The head of another family is a lazy lout who rents out his land allotment just so he can avoid farming it himself,[6] and he drinks with the money his daughter sends home from the city, where she works as a servant. This family of four is always on the brink of starvation, even in a good harvest year. Unproductive peasants of this kind make up at least 10 percent of the village population. And then there is the money that somehow gets "lost" or "stolen" in a tavern, plus expensive customs like the parties thrown for conscripts and the wedding celebrations out of all proportion to people's real means. Compared to these large outlays, four or five extra rubles in taxes are a drop in the bucket. I am not saying that we should abandon efforts to achieve more equitable taxation, but the taxes are, I repeat, literally a drop in the bucket.

[In this connection, it might be pointed out that the liquor merchants are skillful in dealing with their clientele.] When a new tavernkeeper comes to a village, he has to secure a steady flow of customers. To do this he offers to lend peasants from eight to twenty rubles by means of promissory notes that he has notarized

6. Rental might seem to be a business choice, but the rent received was far less than the peasant could earn if he worked the land himself, assuming, of course, that he possessed the livestock and equipment needed for farming.

One of the many peasant crafts. Boys learning the cobbler's trade. Riazan province. Courtesy of the Riazan Museum.

at the township supervisor's office. This is in fact a line of credit extended to peasants by the tavernkeeper, and it is applicable only to purchases made at his establishment: vodka, naturally.[7]

7. While Semyonova may be right about the large outlays for parties and weddings, she seems here more than usual to be judging peasant behavior by the standards of her own educated society and failing to understand the centrality of these activities to family status and community solidarity in the peasant world. This type of display and reaffirmation of community bonds may have been needed more than ever at a time of rapid change, signified by the village's increasing interaction with the city and national government.

10

❖❖❖

COURT CASES AND POLITICAL STRUCTURE

One consequence of the village's increasing interaction with the urban society and the national government was a greater use by the peasants of the courts. Semyonova records a number of typical court cases she observed; she regards the more frequent use of courts by peasants as destructive of community life. Suits were deployed as weapons against persons one disliked or from whom one could expect to gain some monetary advantage. Peasants, of course, were hardly alone in using the courts in this way. The end of serfdom and the accompanying abolition of the legal authority of the serf owner meant that peasants had to find new methods for settling their disputes. The results may have been a messier, more litigious village life, but it was a school in modern institution building as well. Semyonova also remarks on punishments and the peasants' attitudes toward corporal as opposed to monetary penalties. Here we see an example of the continuing power of patriarchal authority in the family and how it affected dependent males as well as females.

Questions of crime and punishment lead to considerations of the political system and government officials and their place in peasant life. Semyonova had something to say about this, too. She notes the influence in village and township governance of kinship networks and bribery, both of which she views with a jaundiced eye. But she does not give enough consideration to the reasons for the existence of these practices; so long as peasants understood authority in personal terms, these practices were no doubt essential to the functioning of local government.

Semyonova's description of the peasants' attitudes toward the township supervisor and the land captain make clear that they did understand authority as personal. They preferred that the person in charge be strong and consistent. Although some peasants resented the manipulation of that authority by others through family connections or bribery, they did not seem to regard this as a flaw in the system. It was perhaps a weakness of a particular man or men, who, if unjust, should be replaced. A system in which power was divided among offices, and in which the occupant of an office was limited to a certain narrow set of decisions, would not have gained the approval of the peasants. They would have had to bribe several people instead of just one in order to get something done or avoid having something unpleasant done to them. Authority, in their view, had to be undivided and personal, like the authority of God or of the tsar, in whom they often placed their hopes for acquisition of the land or the abolition of taxes.

The final story in this chapter reveals that, in addition to the usual complaints about abuses of the community order such as bribery and kin influence, challenges to authority had also begun to reach Semyonova's villages in another, more ominous form: the ideas of urban, middle-class revolutionaries. These ideas had been vigorously proselytized by the revolutionary populists in the 1870s but, according to Semyonova, in those days had not produced a single incident of importance. Now, she feared, a new era had arrived, and she tells of the destruction caused by a peasant farm worker with socialist views around the year 1900. She concludes with a pessimistic remark about the ability of educated people to convert the villagers to a new work ethic, one that would convince them to maximize their earnings and save for the future. But then she wonders whether the people would not justifiably ridicule such advice (as well she might, in view of all the obstacles to economic success she has already described).

CASES HEARD at the township court and resolved on the same day:

1. A peasant sued a brick mason (a specialist in building ovens) for not completing the work by the deadline set in the contract, even though he had already received payment for the job. The jury ruled that the brick mason had to pay the plaintiff for breach of contract. A local landlord, commenting on the case, noted that the plaintiff would not have won if the former way of life and peasant ignorance in legal matters had not recently changed. In earlier days, he would have lost because the bricklayer was also a farmer, and his failure to complete the work on time was a result of the extraordinarily difficult harvest conditions of this year. Had he finished the bricklaying job on time, he might well have lost his own crops, a circumstance that would have provided a basis for acquittal.

2. The younger of two sisters-in-law sued the older one for calling her a slut. This is how it happened. The younger woman had returned with her husband from Novocherkassk, and a short time later her husband and his brother arranged a division of the family property. The younger brother and his wife were unhappy with the amount of land they received, and the women have been quarreling endlessly ever since.

The judge proposed that the two try to make peace. But the younger sister-in-law replied: "I'm not going to make up with her under any circumstances! She called me a tart! This is unheard of! I live with my own husband! I lived six years in Novocherkassk and never heard anything like that from anyone, and then here she goes smarting off!"

Peasants gathered in the street of a village in Tambov province. Photo by S. I. Gerasimova from *Rossiia. Polnoe geograficheskoe opisanie,* vol. 2, p. 175.

The older woman came back: "And why did you call my daughter names first?"

The younger: "She's lying. I never said anything bad to her daughter!"

The older: "Just tell me, why did you call her names? She's a young girl, but even so, I didn't say anything to you about your name calling then. And here you are a grown woman. A few dirty words aren't going to do you any harm. It's not something you take to court. . . . When she got home, everything was waiting for her, full room and board, and what does she say to me?—my fair-minded judges—she says, 'You're completely rotten from lying on the stove.'" And on and on it went.

The upshot was that the jury sentenced the older woman to three days in jail. As she was leaving, she said: "Well, Christ Jesus had to suffer, and so will I." To the amusement of everyone, the younger sister-in-law responded: "What's a mere three days! I would've locked up this martyr for Christ in a dungeon for three years."

3. A woman sued a man for an "estate," a plot of cultivated land. Twelve years ago her late husband exchanged plots with another man from the same village. At that time, the other man had just separated from his family and had still not received his portion of the family property from the village assembly. He paid the woman's husband thirty rubles for a barn that stood on the lot. The agreement they drew up stipulated that although the plot became the property of the new owner, the former owner retained the right to make use of the willows growing on the land until such time as he received from the assembly the plot that originally would have become the property of the new owner. When the woman's husband died, soon after signing the agreement, his partner in the deal had already left for Moscow, taking a copy of the agreement with him. Thus, the widow knew nothing about the exchange. One year after her husband's death, she married a man in another village. When she left, she took her only daughter with her and sold the house. Two years later the new owner of the land returned from Moscow, showed the widow the agreement that he had signed with her late husband, and settled on his new property. Knowing that she could at any time claim from the village assembly the plot due to her according to the agreement, the widow did not bother to file a claim for the time being and continued to live with her new husband. Eleven years after the exchange agreement, the new owner cut down all the willows on the plot and sold them. Then the woman, pursuant to the terms of the agreement that accorded her late husband (and upon his death his daughter, for whom the woman was guardian) use of the willows on the plot, filed a suit against the new owner in the township

court. The man expected to prevail because of the passage of more than ten years since the signing of the agreement, but the court ruled that he had to pay the woman the cost of the willows he had sold.

4. Another case against a peasant who cut down willow trees on his neighbor's land.

5. Litigation between peasants and a landowner. Three peasants undertook (on the basis of joint responsibility) to harvest millet on two desiatinas (5.4 acres) of land for a merchant landowner. While harvesting, one of the peasants quarreled with the merchant and hurled some foul language his way. When the time came to pay up, the merchant deducted fifteen rubles from the crew. The peasants filed a complaint in the township court to reclaim the ten rubles due the two peasants who had not quarreled with the merchant. The merchant failed to appear in court, and the hearing was postponed. It was continued three times for the same reason, and the peasants were angry. "We live far away and have dragged ourselves here for a third time just to find that he hasn't appeared again." The merchant did not come to court because, as a member of the middle class, he was not subject to the jurisdiction of the township court. Unfamiliar with law, the peasants did not know that the case should have been taken not to the township court but to the land captain's court.

There was the following case [in our village]. Two brothers [and their families] lived together [and shared their property]. Then the younger of the two moved to Moscow with his wife. Nothing was heard from him for twenty years, nor did he send any money to his elder brother for household needs. (I should note in this regard that money orders sent home by peasants working elsewhere usually arrive at the office of the township supervisor. The supervisor may arbitrarily retain the money orders to cover taxes owed by peasants, and not even notify the addressees about the arrival of the money. Sometimes he simply pockets the money for himself. In these circumstances, it is difficult to find out whether or not a peasant sent money to his family.) The elder brother kept working on the farm, and after running it for twenty years, he naturally believed the entire property, the house and the land, were his. Then, out of the blue, the younger brother showed up and made threats, demanding not only his share of the land but some of the movable property as well. When his demands were met, he threw a party for the villagers, treating them to vodka, to make sure that they would ratify the property settlement; the village (*mir*) had the right to veto the property division. Then he made himself comfortable "with full room and board," as they say. Obviously, his behavior caused a strong reaction on the part of his brother and his family.

Situations like this are commonly a cause for litigation. In most instances, the argument is over land. But peasants also litigate with landlords over wages, or, more accurately, landlords sue peasants at the land captain's court. Not knowing much about the law, peasants frequently end up suing people who are in the right from the standpoint of the law. Peasants like to go to court, especially when they see an opportunity to gain something from the other party, or to cause someone a lot of trouble for having insulted them. Pointless lawsuits have lately become a bane of peasant life.

Legal Penalties

The common use of corporal punishment, public beatings with birch switches or willow rods, is dying out. Even so, not long ago a woman from a remote village was able to have her husband flogged at the township office for his refusal to live with her. We also continue to see cases of sons being flogged for insulting their parents. These disobedient children (who may be as much as twenty years of age) are taken without trial to the township office for their punishment. In response to a complaint by the parents, the township supervisor summons the son and turns him over to the office guard for flogging. The culprit is stripped from the waist down, placed on the floor in the township office, and beaten with willow rods. Admission to the spectacle is open to all residents of the village.

Peasants resent fines more than beatings or jailing. They view money payments as the harshest punishment and may even revenge themselves with arson. They are much more willing to be locked up, provided it does not occur during the field-work season. If a jail sentence should fall during the time of field work, a peasant may sometimes succeed in persuading the township supervisor to postpone the punishment until the fall. If so, a male relative has to agree to stand surety for the convicted peasant. Vodka naturally plays a major role in such a settlement. "Treat the supervisor and he'll go easy on you," as they say. Women are incarcerated the same as men, and this includes pregnant women and even breast-feeding mothers, who go to jail with their babies in their arms.

When peasants fail to pay their taxes, the township council sends them to jail in another village, ten to twenty miles away, while peasants of the latter village are jailed in the former. Of course, this practice has to be approved by the government land captain.

Local Governance

Peasants tend to think of their village assembly as unjust. "Look how very difficult it is to live in this community. Whoever has the most relatives is right. People will vote for a relative, and then it's hard for those without kin. That is why a peasant without such allies is reluctant to take business to the village assembly. Why bother when they will just vote you down anyhow? And then there's the vodka. With some vodka and money, any judge can be persuaded to declare the guilty party to be in the right."

The person having the greatest sway over the destiny of the village is not the land captain (*zemskii nachal'nik*) but the township supervisor. This is both good and bad. On the one hand, the supervisor is useful to the central government, for he is himself a peasant and knows the inner workings of peasant life that are ultimately beyond the ken of the land captain. On the other hand, the very fact of this special position and his own approach to it as a source of personal enrichment result in much evil.

A supervisor receives a salary of six hundred rubles a year, and therefore is usually able to rent or even own much more land than any other peasant in the village. Naturally, his own interests take priority in any decisions he makes. He also controls the village assembly, taking bribes and locating guzzlers who can be paid off to support him with their votes. These guzzlers can be found in any village. The peasants call them "howlers and gullets." They are "gullets" in the sense that they have large throats for howling and for drinking. These stooges carry even more weight in determining a peasant's fate at the assembly than do his relatives. Behind these stooges is hidden the township supervisor, who, in turn, often represents the interests of a large landowner from the merchant class with capital amounting to a hundred thousand rubles. The supervisor is a frequent guest at the merchant's table, and for a monetary con ideration sees to his patron's interests. He may, for example, press the peasants harder for taxes so that they will be forced to accept low-paying jobs from the merchant. Not long ago one of the supervisors arranged a really remarkable deal for a merchant; he got a peasant community to turn over to the merchant, in exchange for land elsewhere, nearly one hundred acres next to the Purlovo railway station, a site with marvelous possibilities of development, and the merchant had to throw in a mere two thousand rubles extra.

Because of his ability to pay off his stooges, a township supervisor enjoys a secure tenure, and at the end of this three-year term he is reelected. After the election, the peasants who voted against him are likely to suffer when tax-paying time comes. Tax collection normally begins in September, but since the tax applies to the current year, the supervisor can easily demand payment from a peasant one or two months earlier [just when the farmer is busiest and has the least possibility to pay].

In regard to the village assembly, it should be pointed out that peasants do not bother with formal vote counts when they decide on routine matters. They discuss an issue, negotiate back and forth, and then settle on a common position. "Everyone agrees," they announce, and if two or three persons object, no one pays much attention. But in serious matters such as the transfer of land to the merchant mentioned earlier, the supervisor takes a count of the votes, or rather asks the village elder to take it, so as not to be accused of dishonesty. Moreover, in such matters the margin can be very narrow, amounting to only a few votes one way or the other.

The township supervisor is not the only one who accepts bribes. Other officials take them as well; you do not have to look far to find examples. The ordinary peasants, who are oppressed and mistreated and under the thumb of these local representatives of authority, respond as you would expect. After all, they find themselves caught in a vicious circle. In these conditions, who can rise above the general level of misery and set an example for other villagers? The township supervisor is often also the head of the township court. [How then can one appeal his arbitrary decisions even if one had a mind to do so?]

A strong hand on the part of the township supervisor, even the use of corporal punishment, earns the respect of the peasants, provided it is applied consistently. "Our supervisor is really fierce," they will say. "Always greets you with: 'What do ya want, you rascal?' Honest to God, he says that to everyone!" Capricious anger, however, is scorned by peasants. For example, our land captain, basically a "good guy," has fits of rage that alternate with utter weakness. He administers justice when he is drunk and sometimes even deals out blows, but peasants show very little respect for him; they scoff at him.

Socialist Ideas Come to the Village

Aksiuta was a small, dark-eyed orphan girl who had "seen it all." When she was about sixteen, she hired on with a landlord doing general housework—tending the samovar, washing floors, and the like. A year later she announced to the landlord that she wanted to settle up because she had decided to marry a boy of nineteen, who was also an orphan and lived with his uncle. Mikhalek, as the boy was called, had lived in Moscow when he was younger, and then was taken in by his uncle, for whom he worked in exchange for his room and board. Mikhalek was unruly, even somewhat peculiar, and no one had a good word to say about him. The landlord asked Aksiuta why she wanted to marry such a loafer and offered to find her a better match. Aksiuta replied that she could not change her mind, what with her being an orphan, not even having a brother, and said that Mikhalek's uncle would take her into his house. It was clear that she had her mind made up.

Inquiries revealed that some distant relatives of Aksiuta had already tried to prevent the marriage, but to no avail. It also came out that Aksiuta and Mikhalek had long been having intimate relations and had pledged faithfulness to each other. They had even eaten earth to confirm their union. Aksiuta announced that she would marry Mikhalek or no one, preferring otherwise to remain forever single. It turned out that Mikhalek's uncle had encouraged their relationship with the intention of acquiring a free laborer for his household while his own children were growing up. Later he could at any time dismiss the couple.

The wedding took place, a typically poor orphan wedding. The couple lived at the uncle's house for a year, and then Mikhalek found a job working for a landlord. Aksiuta had suffered a miscarriage, very probably self-inflicted, since Mikhalek's uncle would not have let them stay with a baby.

On the landlord's estate where Mikhalek worked, a number of mysterious incidents occurred over the past summer. Several horses and cows died for no apparent reason. The veterinarian could not detect any infections in the animals, but when the hides were removed, the carcasses displayed a black spot at the base of the skull, like a hemorrhage. Besides this, the threshing machine broke on two occasions, the result of iron rods having been intentionally placed in the shocks of grain. Rumors started to circulate among the women who did the threshing that they could next expect to find a box of matches in a shock and then a coupling bolt. It was impossible to get the women to tell who was making these threats. The landlord had not the slightest idea why someone was trying to intimidate him, as he had had no problems with the peasants.

The landlord paid no attention to Mikhalek until the day he

decided to have the young man help him with the work in the garden. They worked together and conversed as a landlord and his hired worker might, but in the course of that ordinary conversation, Mikhalek burst out in a barrage of bitter accusations against "capitalists" [*sic*], rich landowners and rich peasants. "We are homeless and landless, while these rich people plant ornamental gardens and drink tea all day long." (Peasants regard merely decorative gardens, those that bear no fruit, as a foolish and wicked idea, while tea drinking is of course a nice pastime.) Though taken aback at the time, the landlord had many other affairs to attend to and for a time forgot about the incident.

Then, late in the year, during the festival of the village's patron saint (or "feedstival," as the peasants quip), it happened. The harvest had been good, and every last person in the village was drunk. On the third night of the festivities, a barn belonging to a rich village storekeeper caught fire. When the villagers descended on the spot, they found Mikhalek next to the barn and seized him. Meanwhile, the flames reached another barn, and the whole village was in danger of catching fire. No water was available because everything was covered with ice. The peasants (whose stored grain was at stake) all at once fell upon Mikhalek, beat him with whatever they could lay their hands on, and threw him into the fire. He would have burned alive had he not been rescued by the very owner of the barn that he had set on fire. You think the storekeeper was being magnanimous? Not a bit. He was simply afraid that if Mikhalek died in the fire, an investigation would necessarily follow, and the peasants would shift the blame for Mikhalek's death to him, *the victimized wealthy peasant* [italics are Semyonova's]. Although the fire did not spread very far, a few people lost all their grain, and the next day when the constable arrived to investigate, a number of peasants testified that Mikhalek had bragged to them about placing an iron rod in the landlord's threshing machine, about killing several cows belonging to the same landlord, and the like. In other words, as long as only a landlord was being harmed, the peasants who knew what was going on kept quiet and protected "one of their own," even sympathizing with Mikhalek. But the moment they lost their hard-earned possessions, they sang a different tune.

Aksiuta, it turned out, had been helping her husband all along. "He's weird and loutish, but he never beats his wife," or so I heard it said about Mikhalek.

Mikhalek had never had any real disputes with either the wealthy storekeeper or the landlord. He was evidently influenced by some kind of "revolutionary idea." Until this protest emerged, Mikhalek and Aksiuta, both remarkable people with abilities well above those of the average peasant, had quietly borne the burdens of orphanhood and poverty—in fact, it was these circumstances that bound them closely together. It is quite likely that Mikhalek picked up his revolutionary "rhetoric" when he lived in Moscow; that came through pretty clearly in his conversation with the landlord. However unreasonable and rash his actions, they are indicative of the growing hatred of the poor toward the rich and toward large landowners.

Peasants have not acquired the habit of intensive labor, they are deprived of the light of knowledge, and they suffer an oppressive poverty. The problem seems to be that whatever goal a peasant entertains, be it merely the acquisition of a pint of vodka or a pair of galoshes, it is beyond his reach, no matter how hard he works. Another thought that bothers me is how can we, the targets of the people's hatred, alter their goals, open new horizons to them, implant the notion of intensive labor as a source of well-being? They would not believe us and would simply laugh at us, perhaps justifiably.

What is important is that animosity and hatred are on the rise within the peasant population and already, though still rarely, can produce the likes of Mikhalek, who acted on the convictions he came to through his suffering. All the propaganda disseminated by the radical men and women of the 1870s (*semidesiatniki*) who went out and worked among the people, hardly succeeded in producing a single such arsonist.

APPENDIX

Form of a Contract between Seasonal Employers and Peasants

On the 2nd of October, 1899, we, the undersigned peasants of Yepifanskii *uezd* of Murashenskii township and Chernyshevka village, Yakov Matveev Marsakov, Pavel Spiridonov Shikunov, Nikita Pavlov Blagov, and Maksim Grigoriev Seleznyov, have filed this contract with the Karavaevo office of Semyon Tikhonovich Blagopoluchnyi, merchant of the 2nd guild, to the effect that:

1. We, the peasants, have undertaken to farm in the coming year 6 desiatinas of rye and 6 of oats on the estate owned by Semyon Tikhonovich Blagopoluchnyi, merchant of the 2nd guild.

2. For farming these 12 desiatinas we have received upon signing this agreement the entire payment of 5 rubles per desiatina, or 60 rubles in all.

3. Rye will be worked in the following manner: the field is to be plowed and harrowed twice and weeded out. After the rye seeds have been sown, the field is to be harrowed two or three times. Lastly, the rye is to be cut, bound, packed into shocks, transported to the threshing yard, and the ricks covered. Oats will be worked in the following manner: sowing, harrowing twice, weeding, cutting, binding, packing into shocks, transporting to the threshing yard, covering the ricks. In the fall, the field is to be plowed.

4. We pledge not to contract similar jobs. Should we do so, we shall be obliged to pay a penalty of 3 rubles per every forfeited desiatina.

5. For all work, we are to appear when requested and do a good job. The plowing should be done at no less than 8 furrows for each 7 feet. If we fail to appear at the time assigned, we shall do the work at another time and also pay a penalty to the office of S. T.

Blagopoluchnyi in the amount of 2 rubles; or, if we fail to appear at all, we must pay 3 rubles per desiatina. If the plowing is done poorly, we agree to immediately replow the field. Other cases of poor work will entail a fine of 2 rubles per desiatina for each instance. We accept this work as a joint responsibility.

Signatories:	Rye	Oats
Yakov Marsakov	2.0 desiatinas	2.0 desiatinas
Pavel Shikunov	1.5 " "	1.5 " "
Nikita Blagov	1.0 " "	1.0 " "
Maksim Seleznyov	1.5 " "	1.5 " "
Total:	6.0 desiatinas	6.0 desiatinas

Pavel Shikunov is signing this contract for himself and, at their request, for the other signatories, who are illiterate. Signed and sealed on this day the 2nd of October, 1899, at the Murashenskii township office. Township supervisor Stoliarov. Scribe Gruzdkov.

SUGGESTIONS FOR FURTHER READING

Atkinson, Dorothy. *The End of the Russian Land Commune.* Stanford: Stanford University Press, 1985.

Bartlett, Roger, ed. *Land Commune and Peasant Community in Russia: Communal Forms in Imperial and Early Soviet Society.* New York: St. Martin's Press, 1990.

Benet, Sula, ed. *The Village of Viriatino.* New York: Doubleday, 1970.

Bohac, Rodney D. "Peasant Inheritance Strategies in Russia." *Journal of Interdisciplinary History,* 16:1 (1985), 23-42.

Bradley, Joseph. *Muzhik and Muscovite: Urbanization in Late Imperial Russia.* Berkeley: University of California Press, 1985.

Brooks, Jeffrey. *When Russia Learned to Read: Literacy and Popular Literature, 1861-1917.* Princeton: Princeton University Press, 1985.

Bushnell, John. *Mutiny amid Repression: Russian Soldiers in the Revolution of 1905-1906.* Bloomington: Indiana University Press, 1985.

Chayanov, A. V. *The Theory of Peasant Economy* (with a foreword by Teodor Shanin), ed. Daniel Thorner et al. Madison: University of Wisconsin Press, 1986.

Chekhov, Anton. *Peasants and Others Stories.* Trans. Edmund Wilson. New York: Doubleday, 1956.

Clements, Barbara Evans, Barbara Alpern Engel, and Christine D. Worobec, eds. *Russia's Women: Accommodation, Resistance, Transformation.* Berkeley: University of California Press, 1991.

Czap, Peter, Jr. "Marriage and the Peasant Joint Family in the Era of Serfdom." In *The Family in Imperial Russia,* ed. David L. Ransel. Urbana: University of Illinois Press, 1978.

Dunn, Stephen, and Ethel Dunn. *The Peasants of Central Russia.* New York: Waveland, 1988.

Edelman, Robert. *Proletarian Peasants: The Revolution of 1905 in Russia's Southwest.* Ithaca: Cornell University Press, 1987.

Eklof, Ben. *Russian Peasant Schools: Officialdom, Village Culture, and Popular Pedagogy, 1861-1914.* Berkeley: University of California Press, 1986.

———. "Ways of Seeing: Recent Anglo-American Studies of the Russian Peasant (1861-1914)." *Jahrbücher für Geschichte Osteuropas,* 36:1 (1988), 57-79.

Eklof, Ben, and Stephen P. Frank, eds. *The World of the Russian Peasant: Post-Emancipation Culture and Society.* Boston: Unwin Hyman, 1990.

Emmons, Terence, ed. *The Emancipation of the Russian Serfs.* New York: Holt, Rinehart and Winston, 1970.

Emmons, Terence, and Wayne Vucinich, eds. *The Zemstvo in Russia: An Experiment in Local Self-Government.* Cambridge: Cambridge University Press, 1982.

Engelstein, Laura. "Morality and the Wooden Spoon: Russian Doctors View Syphilis, Social Class, and Sexual Behavior, 1890-1905," *Representations,* 14 (Spring 1981), 169-208.

Farnsworth, Beatrice. "The Litigious Daughter-in-Law: Family Relations in Rural Russia in the Second Half of the Nineteenth Century." *Slavic Review,* 45:1 (1986), 49-64.

———. "The Soldatka: Folklore and Court Record." *Slavic Review,* 49:1 (1990), 58-73.

Field, Daniel. *Rebels in the Name of the Tsar.* Boston: Unwin and Hyman, 1975.

Frank, Stephen P. *Cultural Conflict, Law, and Criminality in Rural Russia, 1861-1907.* Forthcoming.

Freeze, Gregory L. *The Parish Clergy in the Nineteenth Century: Crisis, Reform and Counter-Reform.* Princeton: Princeton University Press, 1983.

Frierson, Cathy. "Rural Justice in Russia: The Volost' Court Debate, 1861-1912." *Slavonic and East European Review,* 64 (October 1986).

Hoch, Steven L. *Serfdom and Social Control in Russia: Petrovskoe, a Village in Tambov.* Chicago: University of Chicago Press, 1986.

Ivanits, Linda J. *Russian Folk Belief.* Armonk, N.Y.: M. E. Sharpe, 1989.

Johnson, Robert E. *Peasant and Proletarian: The Working Class of Moscow in the Late Nineteenth Century.* New Brunswick, N.J.: Rutgers University Press, 1979.

Kanatchikov, S. *A Radical Worker in Tsarist Russia: The Autobiography of Semen Ivanovich Kanatchikov.* Trans. and ed. Reginald E. Zelnik. Stanford: Stanford University Press, 1986.

Kingston-Mann, Esther, and Timothy Mixter, eds. *Peasant Economy, Culture, and Politics of European Russia, 1800-1921.* Princeton: Princeton University Press, 1991.

Kolchin, Peter. *Unfree Labor: American Slavery and Russian Serfdom.* Cambridge, Mass.: Harvard University Press, 1987.

Krukones, James H. *To the People: The Russian Government and the Newspaper "Selskii Vestnik" ("Village Herald"), 1881-1917.* New York: Garland, 1987.

Macey, David A. J. *Government and Peasant in Russia, 1861-1906: The Pre-history of the Stolypin Reforms.* Dekalb: Northern Illinois University Press, 1987.

Pallot, Judith, and Denis J. B. Shaw. *Landscape and Settlement in Romanov Russia.* New York: Oxford University Press, 1990.

Ransel, David L., ed. *The Family in Imperial Russia: New Lines of Historical Research.* Urbana: University of Illinois Press, 1978.

———. *Mothers of Misery: Child Abandonment in Russia.* Princeton: Princeton University Press, 1988.

Robbins, Richard G., Jr. *Famine in Russia, 1891-1892*. New York: Columbia University Press, 1975.

Robinson, Geroid Tanquary. *Rural Russia under the Old Regime*. Berkeley: University of California Press, 1969.

Seregny, Scott. *Russian Teachers and Peasant Revolution: The Politics of Education in 1905*. Bloomington: Indiana University Press, 1989.

Shanin, Teodor. *The Awkward Class: Political Sociology of Peasantry in a Developing Society, Russia, 1910-1925*. Oxford: Oxford University Press, 1972.

———. *The Roots of Otherness: Russia's Turn of the Century*. Vol. 1: *Russia as a "Developing Society"*; vol. 2: *Russia, 1905-07: Revolution as a Moment of Truth*. New Haven: Yale University Press, 1985.

Shinn, William T., Jr. "The Law of the Russian Peasant Household." *Slavic Review*, 20:4 (1961), 601-21.

Treadgold, Donald W. *The Great Siberian Migration: Government and Peasant in Resettlement from Emancipation to the First World War*. Princeton: Princeton University Press, 1957.

Vucinich, Wayne S., ed. *The Peasant in Nineteenth-Century Russia*. Stanford: Stanford University Press, 1968.

Weissman, Neil. "Rural Crime in Tsarist Russia: The Question of Hooliganism, 1905-1914." *Slavic Review*, 37:2 (1978), 228-40.

Wilbur, Elvira M. "Was Russian Peasant Agriculture Really That Impoverished? New Evidence from a Case Study from the 'Impoverished Center' at the End of the 19th Century." *Journal of Economic History*, 43:1 (1983), 137-44.

Wirtschafter, Elise Kimerling. *From Serf to Russian Soldier*. Princeton: Princeton University Press, 1990.

Worobec, Christine D. *Peasant Russia: Family and Community in the Post-Emancipation Period*. Princeton: Princeton University Press, 1991.

Yaney, George. *The Urge to Mobilize: Agrarian Reform in Russia, 1861-1930*. Urbana: University of Illinois Press, 1982.

Zelnik, Reginald E. *Labor and Society in Tsarist Russia: The Factory Workers of St. Petersburg, 1855-1870*. Stanford: Stanford University Press, 1971.

DAVID L. RANSEL is Professor of History and Adjunct Professor of Women's Studies at Indiana University. Formerly editor of the *Slavic Review* and currently editor of the *American Historical Review*, Ransel has published extensively on topics of Russian political and social history. He is author of *The Politics of Catherinian Russia* and *Mothers of Misery: Child Abandonment in Russia* and editor of *The Family in Imperial Russia: New Lines of Historical Research*.

CPSIA information can be obtained
at www.ICGtesting.com
Printed in the USA
JSHW011715140723
44606JS00009B/61
9 780253 207845